"For forty-four years, Larry Spencer left his leadership imprint on our Air Force and everyone he met. Now *Dark Horse* allows an even broader audience to learn from this remarkably successful, positive, humble, caring leader. A truly inspirational read!"

—**Gen. Martin Dempsey (Ret.)**
18th Chairman of the Joint Chiefs of Staff

"In the Black Lives Matter era, General Spencer's memoir is timely and instructive. His vivid prose puts the reader at his side, watching events through his eyes as he experienced a wide variety of situations. His achievements in overcoming negative peer pressure, low expectations, racial stereotypes, and discrimination can serve as an inspiration for many Americans."

—**Paul Stillwell**
Editor of *The Golden Thirteen: Recollections of the First Black Naval Officers*

"Larry Spencer has been a true leader in his life's work, making our armed forces stronger and more effective. *Dark Horse* shares the secrets of his success: his dedication to duty and his innate decency. His life is a valuable lesson for us all as we work to make America the best it can be."

—**Sheryl Sandberg**
Chief Operating Officer of Facebook, founder of Lean In and Option B

"Gen. Larry Spencer left his mark on the United States Air Force and now he does so again with this timely, relevant, and extremely important book, which also provides a needed addition to USAF history. General Spencer has written an earnest and intimate portrait that covers valuable perspectives from both his enlisted and officer career. Detailing issues of racial strife, overcoming adversity, and filled with lessons in leadership, Spencer writes with ineffable grace, wit, and charm. Leaders at all levels should read this book, to steal a phrase from General Spencer, with 'eagerness and enthusiasm.'"

—**Dr. Brian D. Laslie**
Command Historian, United States Air Force Academy

DARK HORSE

DARK HORSE

General Larry O. Spencer
and His Journey from
the Horseshoe to
the Pentagon

General Larry O. Spencer, USAF (Ret.)

NAVAL INSTITUTE PRESS
Annapolis, Maryland

Naval Institute Press
291 Wood Road
Annapolis, MD 21402

Library of Congress Cataloging–in–Publication Data
Names: Spencer, Larry O., date– author.
Title: Dark horse : General Larry O. Spencer and his journey from the Horseshoe to the
    Pentagon / General Larry O. Spencer, USAF (Ret.).
Other titles: General Larry O. Spencer and his journey from the Horseshoe to the Pentagon
Description: Annapolis, Maryland : Naval Institute Press, [2021] | Includes bibliographical
    references.
Identifiers: LCCN 2021025101 (print) | LCCN 2021025102 (ebook) |
    ISBN 9781682477021 (hardcover) | ISBN 9781682477045 (ebook) |
    ISBN 9781682477045 (pdf)
Subjects: LCSH: Spencer, Larry O., 1953– | United States. Air Force—Officers—
    Biography. | United States. Air Force—African Americans—History. | African
    American generals—Biography. | Generals—United States—Biography. | United States.
    Air Force—Military life—History—20th century. | Washington (D.C.)—Biography.
Classification: LCC E897.4.S64 A3 2021 (print) | LCC E897.4.S64 (ebook) |
    DDC 358.40092 [B]—dc23
LC record available at https://lccn.loc.gov/2021025101
LC ebook record available at https://lccn.loc.gov/2021025102

♾ This paper meets the requirements of ANSI/NISO z39.48-1992 (Permanence of Paper).
Printed in the United States of America.

29 28 27 26 25 24 23 22 21   9 8 7 6 5 4 3 2 1
First printing

Contents

☆ ☆ ☆ ☆

Preface

☆ ☆ ☆ ☆

There is no greater agony than bearing
an untold story inside of you.

—MAYA ANGELOU[1]

On September 9, 1953, I came into existence as a dark horse, a contender with little or no chance of succeeding. Born an African American in the early 1950s on a tough inner-city southeast Washington, D.C., street called the Horseshoe, made me a dark horse. Dad was an enlisted man in the U.S. Army and worked two jobs to support our family of eight. Neighborhood kids teased me because Dad wore a prosthetic hook in place of his amputated left hand, an injury he received during the Korean War. Mom had not completed high school and had no driver's license. Both had migrated from southern Virginia, where Jim Crow laws and the separate-but-equal doctrine dominated their early lives and shaped their life perspective.

We shared our nine-hundred-square-foot duplex home with roaches and mice. I walked to school each day with my head on a swivel in close watch for an unprovoked fight. I was a poor student in school. I was trapped inside a cocoon of low self-esteem and poor self-worth. Teachers passed me along to the next grade with the hope I would do better. If they only knew how desperately I wanted to do better. I needed help. I needed guidance. I needed a mentor, but there were none. Positive role models were few, and negative images and stereotypes were abundant. As an introvert, I felt isolated. My outlook for a meaningful future was desolate.

I had many personal struggles during my youth. I struggled to make sense of a society that labeled me a "minority," or worse. I didn't understand how skin color could determine one's future. My escape from a lack of hope was food, so I struggled with my weight and self-image. The neighborhood kids called me "fat boy." Worse, some of my family ridiculed me over my appearance. Only in hindsight do I understand their intentions were pure, but at the time the pain of the personal derision was indescribably deep. I don't blame them now. I refuse to believe they knew how I cringed when I was compared with relatives they felt I should be more like. But during my youth, the constant expressions of repulsion were like a dagger in my spirit.

Sports ruled on the Horseshoe. As a young African American male, being good at sports was expected, and I was good. Rain or shine, I played football and basketball every day. My dream was to play in the National Football League; that was supposed to be my ticket out of the Horseshoe. For me, like most of my friends, that ticket never got punched. In stark contrast, academic acuity was eschewed and those who excelled in school were accused of acting white. Fighting also ruled in my neighborhood, and I had my share of fights, some triumphant and others not. Negotiation and compromise were viewed as weak. Those not skilled with their fists were labeled "punks" and faced the scorn of neighborhood bullies.

There was little disposable income in the home, so if I wanted money I had to earn it. I developed a knack and a passion for saving money and seeking efficiency. I hung on for dear life to the back of a city trash truck collecting garbage. I stripped and waxed floors in a department store. I delivered newspapers on my paper route for the *Washington Post* and now-defunct *Washington News*. I cut grass, washed cars, and shoveled snow in winter for neighbors on the Horseshoe. I set up my own lemonade stand and was robbed on the very first day.

I witnessed a host of significant events during my lifetime that molded and shaped who I am today. As a kid, I attended the Martin Luther King Jr. March on Washington in 1963. I watched the Beatles perform on *The Ed Sullivan Show* in 1964. I watched Walter Cronkite report body counts from the Vietnam War on the evening news. I watched the burning of my city of birth following the tragic assassination of Martin Luther King Jr. in 1968. That same year, I watched Mom cry the day Senator Robert "Bobby" Kennedy was murdered. I witnessed the genius of Jimi Hendrix at Woodstock in 1969. I watched in horror as Ohio National Guardsmen shot and killed four unarmed students protesting at Kent State University.

Two significant events changed my life trajectory. First, and quite by chance, I enlisted in the U.S. Air Force. That event was neither planned nor anticipated and is inexplicable even today. Second, while enlisted in the Air Force I obtained my college degree. I have since been told that education is the great equalizer. For me, obtaining a bachelor of science degree was more than an equalizer—it was a life-altering event. Enlisting in the Air Force took me out of the neighborhood and mental captivity that I believed offered no escape. Through the Air Force, I lost weight, gained confidence, and discovered an innate talent to lead.

Obtaining a college degree opened a world for me that I could not imagine. A degree gave me a sense of self-worth I didn't believe existed. I discovered I was as smart as anyone else and in some cases maybe smarter. A college degree provided the opportunity to become a commissioned Air Force officer, which placed me in positions of responsibility. It afforded me influence and credibility. Whereas my enlisted years allowed me to run, becoming an officer allowed me to soar high above a life that I wanted so desperately to leave behind, to accomplish things my parents could not even dream about. Over time, with God's help, I was able to achieve what most believed was unachievable.

My life journey and my Air Force career were anything but orthodox and were not a blueprint I would recommend to others. I had to overcome a substandard inner-city educational system to eventually attend classes at Harvard University. As an airman, I endured the racial tensions of the 1970s. I had to compete for senior Air Force positions that were previously dominated by pilots and considered unattainable for a career financial manager. I took on tough, critical jobs that no one of color had held before. I supported three major wars. My journey was uphill, to be sure, but I thrived on the climb.

I began my Air Force journey as an airman, pay grade E-1. I entered military service having barely graduated from high school. I retired from the Air Force as a four-star general with two master's degrees. In my youth, one of my first jobs was slinging large trash containers into the smelly hull of a trash compactor. My final job in the Air Force was vice chief of staff, the second-highest-ranking military member in the Air Force. In my youth, I was one of a million inner-city kids on a road to nowhere. In the Air Force, I was one of only nine African American four-star generals in Air Force history and one of two African American four-stars who was not a pilot. I was and continue to be the only Air Force officer in Air Force history with a primary career area of financial management to be promoted to four stars.

Throughout those years I had many people suggest that I write about my experiences to serve as motivation for others. That was a humbling consideration that gave me pause, because I did not think my journey was worthy of inspiration. After speaking publicly about my life experiences, however, it was evident I had a story others wanted to hear. I have had thousands of people tell me my life experience now serves as motivation for them. I have had hundreds of airmen say they want to follow in my footsteps. Those comments are sobering and certainly not deserved, but if writing about my life experience can help just one person, I am honored to record my journey. There are many people who I call friends who think they know who I am. In reality, they have no idea about the challenges of a once–dark horse who endured and thrived on a journey from the Horseshoe to the Pentagon.

1

THE HORSESHOE

I am a reflection of my community.

—TUPAC SHAKUR[1]

It was my first day in junior high school, and I was sweating bullets. I learned to trash talk like everyone else in the neighborhood and even had a few brief skirmishes. But a real public fight, never. My stomach churned over the conflicts going through my head. The conflicts of not wanting to fight versus looking like a punk in front of my friends. In my neighborhood, there was no worse label than that of a punk. It meant you were scared. It meant you were weak. It meant you were soft. Above all, wearing that label would make one a prime target of neighborhood bullies.

It was gym class at John Philip Sousa Junior High School, an all-black school in southeast D.C. An older teenager, trying to impress his friends, walked up to me and said, "Punk, get out of my way," and shoved me to the side. At once I had a dilemma. My mind and my heart wanted to simply give him space and move on. But my pride had a different idea. As a small crowd gathered, in the heat of the moment, my pride pushed ahead, and I said, "No, punk, you move." Those four words escaped through my lips before reason could intercede. That short but formidable statement put my existence into suspended animation. As my heartbeat quickened, the crowd grew larger and louder as my opponent pushed me again.

Subconsciously, I knew the right thing was to walk away, but the pressure of backing down in front of what seemed like the entire student body was too intense.

If I walked away now, I could not face my friends. This was bigger than me. This was my reputation as well as the reputation of my neighborhood on the line. As I regained my balance, my opponent laughed, thinking that I would certainly not tangle with an older student. Guided mostly by fear and without calculation, eyes closed, I clenched my fist and swung as hard as I could, and I landed a punch squarely on his jaw. The sound of my fist connecting with his face startled me. It is a sound that movie special effects don't quite capture. I had never punched anyone in the face before, and I didn't like it. I desperately wanted to take back my thoughtless overreaction, but it was too late. I had just entered into an abyss with no predictable end.

The crowd erupted in a chorus of "ooooohhh," followed by a pregnant pause as they became transfixed on my opponent's next move. The look on his face said it all. He was stunned and in disbelief as he gathered himself for battle. I instinctively raised my hands up to the fighting position when, lucky for me, our grizzled and very large gym teacher stepped between us and broke up the fight and the crowd. My sense of relief was palpable as my trash talking was silenced. Conversely, my shaken opponent was boiling mad. I had embarrassed him in front of his "boys." Despite the presence of our gym teacher, he yelled out that he would see me after school to finish the fight. That very public threat launched me into an impenetrable fog. Rumors of the impending fight spread like wildfire, and nothing got our student body animated more than talk of an after-school fight.

The more talk I heard about the fight, the more I panicked. I concocted a scheme to fake an illness to leave school early. I visited the school clinic, but despite my accelerated pulse, my temperature was normal and there were no visible signs of illness, so the nurse sent me back to class. I seriously considered finding my opponent and quietly apologizing, but word would certainly get out that I backed down. The truth is, I wanted to back down. The truth is, I had never been more afraid in my life. Just up the street from our school was an area where after-school fights took place. I had witnessed many fights there but never thought I would be in the actual arena.

I toyed with the idea of taking an alternate route home. I knew full well, however, that my neighborhood friends would see right through that scheme and expose the gripping fear I felt inside. Most school days always dragged on forever, but on this day the school bell marking the end of the day came all too soon. I was so anxious I could hardly breathe. My heart was pounding. I tried to maintain a calm outer demeanor but inside I was nauseated. As I walked out of the school entrance and headed along my normal route home, I noticed a few students gathering around the after-school fight area in anticipation. My mind raced as I played out the fight scene in my mind. Would his punches hurt? Would I cry in front of the crowd? How would the fight start? How would the fight end?

As I continued up the hill, my anxiety eased a bit, as I could not locate my opponent. Could this be true? Was this "smack talking" upperclassman as terrified as I was? Whatever the reason, my opponent did not show. With a brief prayer of thanks, I ignored the crowd, quickened my step, and hurried home. The next day, my opponent and I briefly crossed paths, but neither of us said a word. It was obvious to me he did not want to fight, and I assume it was just as obvious to him that I wanted to move on as well. Fortune was with me for my first fight in the "hood." Unfortunately, I wasn't so lucky during subsequent encounters.

As a dark horse, I entered the race of life with no definitive path for success. Life as an African American during the 1950s and 1960s was tough. As a black youth, I felt devalued. Those blacks deemed successful by society were entertainers or professional athletes, so I chose to be a professional athlete. Adults in the neighborhood complained about working hard every day but never getting ahead. Yet we all witnessed pimps and numbers runners driving fancy cars and dressed to the nines. Attending school each day was something I did, not a means to an end. Life did not exist outside my neighborhood, and I felt confined. That confinement was socioeconomic and emotional rather than physical. Yet that was my life and the life of my friends on the Horseshoe.

The Horseshoe

Forty-Sixth Place in southeast Washington, D.C., is literally shaped like a horseshoe. For those familiar with the city, Forty-Sixth Place is about a mile and a half south of the infamous Shrimp Boat, a landmark restaurant built the year I was born. My father, Alfonzo, was born on a farm in Red House, Virginia, in 1927. Like his brother before him and his brothers that followed, to escape the farm, young Alfonzo enlisted in the U.S. Army immediately following high school in 1946. During the Korean War, Dad earned a Purple Heart when his left hand was amputated due to wounds he suffered. Despite his handicap, he remained in the Army for a full career.

My mother, Selma, was born in 1934 in her home in Cullen, Virginia, although the specific date is in some dispute. My grandmother told Mom her birthday was

September 4, 1934, which is the date she celebrated every year. However, at age seventeen, when Mom requested her birth certificate, the date showed August 3, 1934. Speculation is that the midwife that assisted with her birth simply made a mistake when recording her birth date at the local courthouse. Mom remained resolute that her mother was the ultimate authority; so while her official birthdate displayed on her social security card, taxes, driver's license, and so on, still shows August 3, she continues to celebrate her birth in September.

Dad purchased our house on the Horseshoe in 1955 for $13,500. At the time, he felt the $75 monthly payments were outrageous. He also hated the nineteen-mile one-way commuting distance to work at Forest Glen, Maryland, which was an annex to Walter Reed Army Medical Center, where Dad recovered from his war injury. Given that the monthly basic pay for an E-4 in 1955 was $159.90, I certainly sympathize with his displeasure. On the other hand, with gas at twenty-nine cents per gallon, the tradeoff of driving distance and mortgage payment was a good deal for the times. Mom had researched homes closer to Forest Glen. She was impressed with the school system in Montgomery County, Maryland. At the time, though, real estate agents would not show those homes to "colored" families and, as she rationalized, they "could not afford to live there anyway."

The Horseshoe is lined with brick duplex homes with three levels. Including all three floors, the square footage totaled about nine hundred feet. If you stretched out your arms, your palms would nearly touch each side of the walls in the very small, bowling-lane-shaped kitchen. Mousetraps lined the floor under the sink, and small brown roaches scurried along the tabletops and inside the cabinets. We watched a twelve-inch, black-and-white television with "rabbit ear" antennas, and there was a small but noisy portable air conditioning unit in the front living room window. While watching TV one evening, I told Mom that something had just run across the room. She looked over at me and casually answered, "Don't worry, it's just mice."

Our family of eight shared three small bedrooms and a single bathroom on the upper level. I shared a room with my three brothers, Leland, Keith, and Charles (nicknamed Mutt). We slept on two bunk beds and there was a single dresser for clothes. My sisters, Robin and Kate, shared the second small bedroom. My parents' bedroom was at the front of the house and, as was the fashion of the time (established by the *I Love Lucy* show during the 1950s), had two single beds. Our home had a small front yard with a cement front porch where neighbors sat in the evenings and talked across the chain link fence. The backyard, where my siblings and I played and where Mom hung freshly washed clothes to dry, was a bit larger.

On a gorgeous day when I was five, Mom called me in for lunch. I gulped down my bologna sandwich quickly so I could head back outdoors to play. With the last bite of my sandwich still in my mouth, I charged full speed toward the front door, which was open, exposing the glass storm door. As I had done a hundred times before, I raised my right hand to push the door handle, but this time the glass door was locked. My momentum carried me right through the glass door and onto the concrete front porch. Mom, terrified by the sound of shattering glass, raced to my rescue. When she reached me I was lying on the front porch, bleeding and covered with glass. Miraculously, other than a few cuts and bruises, I was not seriously injured. Dad, however, was not amused when he arrived home from work to find the broken front door.

Despite its modest size, our house was the hub of activity for relatives and friends. Uncles, aunts, and cousins were constant fixtures during weekends and holidays. While my extended paternal and maternal families were influential in my upbringing, they could not have been more dissimilar. Mom's family members were expressive, and their bid whist card games in our living room were legendary and filled with trash talk. They were raised poor but were full of life and laughter. My Uncle Jim worked as a janitor in a department store, my Aunt Ruth worked as a maid, and my Uncle Leroy worked in a liquor store. Despite their modest economic means, they were fun to be around and role models that I admired greatly.

Although Dad's family was also raised with little income, their farm produced most of what they needed. Dad's siblings were generally more formally educated and were raised with a strong work ethic by my authoritarian grandfather. Several of my aunts attended college while my uncles all entered the military. My Aunt Ginny was a nurse and my Aunt Faye was an educator. My Uncle Andrew rose to the top enlisted rank of E-9 in the U.S. Army, and Uncle James served in the U.S. Navy before working more than thirty years for Bethlehem Steel Corporation in Baltimore. Although they were also fun to be around, they were more stoic than Mom's siblings, a trait I inherited. Among the sea of negative images I endured in my youth, those family gatherings provided a much-needed refuge.

Growing up, Dad never told me he loved me or otherwise expressed feelings or emotion. His own upbringing, which was mostly influenced by his father, conditioned him to be this way, as Dad conditioned me. Some of my siblings were bothered by his lack of personal expression, but I was not. As a parent, I came to realize that parents and their offspring often have unrealistic expectations of each other. Family life is often portrayed in movies or television as void of imperfection. I've come to realize there is no perfect parent or perfect child, and everyone is different. And I suppose being an introvert helped me understand that people are often misunderstood, and for some, expressing personal feelings, even to a parent or child, is really difficult. I never had doubts about Dad's caring and desire for all his offspring to do well in life, so my approach was to cut him a break. Besides, it's easy for me to say Dad never said he loved me, because I realize I never said those words to him.

Clearly, the loss of Dad's left hand during the Korean War was a significant event in his life. Yet he never discussed the circumstances surrounding the injury. To his credit, he never let his handicap limit any of his activities, including tossing around a football or baseball with me in the backyard. I don't know if he felt inadequate when he mishandled a fast pitch or struggled to throw a perfect football spiral, but he never once let the loss of an extremity limit his life or his activities with his family.

Dad tried his best to attend most of my sports events at school. He occasionally brought with him one of his best friends from his Army service, Mr. George Crocker, who was a great family friend and role model. A special treat was the rare occasion when we attended a professional football or baseball game. Dad was a huge Washington Redskins (now Washington Football Team) fan, and I enjoyed watching him cheer and interact with fellow fans. An oddity for me was to watch him drink the pocketful of miniature liquor bottles that he referred to as "antifreeze" for the cold temperatures. Likewise, his explanation for paying exorbitant prices for beer during Washington Senators baseball games was that they helped him stay cool during the warm temperatures.

The loss of Dad's left hand affected more than his ability to throw a ball. Throughout my entire childhood, when neighborhood friends asked why my Dad wore a prosthetic hook in place of his hand, I was ashamed to tell the truth, which was that I didn't have a clue. Instead, I made up elaborate stories that would rival some of the most famous war scenes in a movie. As a youngster, having a Dad with a missing hand and not knowing the circumstances surrounding the loss was difficult and confusing—so much so that at twelve years old in 1965, when my mother was pregnant with my youngest sister Kate, I was too embarrassed to ask Mom if Kate would be born missing her left hand.

Similarly, Mom rarely expressed words of tenderness or support. My siblings and I understood that both parents loved us, but the actual words were not spoken.

I sensed that Mom wanted a more expressive and communicative family dynamic, but like Dad, she had never experienced those kinds of family interactions growing up. With six children it was all she could do to keep her own head above water. In addition to serving on active duty as an Army soldier, Dad worked a part-time job as a bartender at the Enlisted Club, so since Mom did not have a driver's license, she was essentially isolated on the Horseshoe all day with the six of us.

My parents never talked to me about sex, or anything else of real consequence. Mirroring their own upbringings, they believed children should not be involved with "grown folks" business. As the oldest, I probably spent the most alone time with Dad since we both enjoyed fishing and sports. Waking at 3:00 a.m. we made the three-hour drive to the Delaware coast along with several of his friends. Following another two-hour boat ride into the ocean, we fished the entire day. The trash talk and profane language between him and his friends was enough to make a sailor blush. Our time spent fishing and attending sporting events, however, represented the most real conversation we had.

As an introvert, the basement in our house was my solace and where I spent hours listening to the "Motown Sound" on my small transistor radio. A wall separated the rear area of the basement that contained a washing machine and workbench. I can still remember the sound of the swish-swash of the 1940s vintage Maytag wringer machine. Mom hand-fed the washed clothes through the rolling pin–like wringers that squeezed out the excess water. She then carefully guided the damp clothes into a plastic basket on the floor. When the wash was complete, she hung the clothes on a clothesline in the backyard and secured them with small wooden clothespins until dry, where more than once, our clothes were stolen right off the clothesline, clothespins and all. The final stage was hours of ironing and pressing to make hand-me-down clothes look good as new.

Inner-City Blues

Activity on the Horseshoe was constant. Young girls jumped double-dutch rope and played hopscotch on the sidewalk. Boys played sports in the street during the day and hung out on the corner at night. No one wanted to miss the weekend house parties where the latest Motown sounds would spin on 45-rpm records. During summer months the jingle of the ice cream truck was like an elixir for those with ten cents to spend. When temperatures really got hot, the older kids would use a large wrench to "pop" open a fire hydrant so the younger kids could run through the strong, steady stream of water. Dogs fighting in the street were common, and cats of unknown origin were abundant.

"Joanin'," or talking trash to each other, was a popular pastime on the Horseshoe. When things got really serious, the old reliable refrain, "yo' momma," was pulled out of reserve. In hindsight, I suppose it was an early form of rapping because "spitting" poetic and rhythmic rhymes about one's looks, habits, or family members was a true art form and mostly good-natured. But things could quickly get heated if someone felt particularly offended. Joanin' was particularly painful for me because of the prosthetic hook Dad wore. Kids can be cruel, but the "Captain Hook" jokes about an injury Dad suffered while serving in the Korean War were particularly harsh and hurtful.

Sports and music dominated life on the Horseshoe, and, unfortunately, academic prowess took a back seat. As a young black kid, being good at sports was expected, and achieving academic success would get one labeled a nerd or the accusation of acting white, which in hindsight was an absurdity. Hall of Fame basketball player Kareem Abdul-Jabbar experienced this firsthand. In his book *Giant Steps*, he described the reaction of his peers at his all-black boarding school just outside of Philadelphia. "I got all A's and was hated for it; I spoke correctly and was called a punk. I had to learn a new language simply to be able to deal with the threats. I had good manners and was a good little boy and paid for it with my hide."[2]

My friends and I played football or basketball every day, rain or shine. For basketball, there was no rim on the Horseshoe to shoot at; rather, shooting the ball just above a thin tin identification strip on the wooden telephone wire posts scored two points. Touch football was played in the narrow street, causing parents, especially my dad, great angst when the ball hit or otherwise landed on their vehicle.

From my early youth, my goal was to be a National Football League (NFL) player. Every day after school I could not wait to get home, change clothes, and head outside to play. As I ventured into other sports, such as basketball, I found I had a natural ability to perform well. I frequently daydreamed of catching the winning touchdown pass in the Super Bowl or scoring the winning basket as time ticked away during the National Basketball Association (NBA) finals. Unfortunately, I did not fare as well academically in school. I could not recite my multiplication tables, but I memorized most of the NFL players on each team. This lack of academic success started at a young age and continued throughout my secondary school tenure.

In the fall of 1959, at age six, I entered the first grade at Davis Elementary School, which was a short ten-minute walk from the Horseshoe. The school was overcrowded, and the books were worn and tattered. Even in a school system not known for its academic achievement I was behind the classroom curriculum from the start. Since Mom had not graduated from high school and Dad worked two jobs, I lacked the preschool training that the school assumed I had obtained. I specifically remember an elementary school assignment to write my first book report. It was the children's book *Green Eggs and Ham*, by Dr. Seuss. I had never written a book report before and had no idea how to proceed. Exasperated, using my best handwriting, I simply copied the words verbatim from several pages. My teacher felt sorry for me and gave me a "D" instead of the "F" I deserved, which left me frustrated and embarrassed.

In other cases, I secretly cried when fellow students displayed interesting and thought-provoking science projects that made my submissions pale in comparison. I desperately wanted to make my teachers and parents proud, but I lacked the study habits and academic acuity to do so. Oftentimes, I surmised and rationalized that I was simply not smart. To make matters worse, my parents assumed that laziness was the primary culprit behind my lack of academic success. Confused and frustrated by my poor grades, my parents defaulted to the only option they knew: a "whipping" with a belt. They told me I could get good grades if I wanted to but they failed to recognize that a lack of effort was not the root cause. While I desperately needed tutoring and self-confidence, at the time I did not know how to articulate those deficiencies.

During a parent-teacher conference, my teachers recommended holding me back a year in elementary school. In hindsight, that was sound advice, but at the time I wanted no part of it. Many of my friends had been held back in school and the ridicule and scorn they suffered on the Horseshoe was brutal and relentless. Students held back a grade were called stupid and dumb, and at that young age I could not imagine anything worse. So, as an alternative, I was forced to attend summer school to make up for my lack of academic performance. Unfortunately, the six-mile city bus ride to summer school was of little consequence as the teachers hated being in a hot classroom with no air conditioning even worse than the students did. As a result, I checked the box of attendance but learned very little.

"Thou Shalt Not Steal"

Unfortunately, my frustration with school caused me to act out. Despite the whippings for poor school grades, I began hanging out with a group of boys who were constantly looking for trouble. Only in hindsight did I realize that what drew us together was they lacked the same basic academic skills and self-esteem that I did.

I learned at a young age that I could get away with more mischief when Dad was not around. So when Dad worked late nights on Monday, Wednesday, and Friday, I took advantage of his absence to hang out with my friends on the corner much later than he would have allowed. One wintry Friday evening around 7:00 p.m. my friends and I hatched a plan to score some snacks for the weekend.

The plan was to enter a local corner store, have my friends distract the store manager, stuff as many candy bars into my coat pockets as possible, and make an easy getaway. This seemed perfectly logical to me, except I privately wondered why they picked me to carry out the most dubious part of the plan. This was the early 1960s, so unlike the quick in-and-out convenience stores today, this old corner variety store featured a grill, magazine rack, a row of pay telephone booths, and a variety of on-the-shelf food items. I had frequented the store many times so the store manager acknowledged me as I entered.

Just like we planned, my friends entered behind me and asked the store manager for a menu from the grill. That was my cue to start grabbing as many snacks as I could stuff in my winter coat. Since this was a first for me, I did not notice several carefully placed large round mirrors that allowed the manager full view of the store. And, as I discovered years later in a conversation with the store manager, he had seen this type of buffoonery before, so he was wise to our plan.

Coat pockets bulging, I sheepishly moved toward the exit door when the store manager stepped in front of me and asked that I empty my pockets. At that moment, the thought occurred to me that my friends and I had no alternate plan. So I did what came naturally at the time and made up a lie. I initially explained to the store manager that I had the money but simply forgot to pay. When the store manager walked me back to the cash register, however, I could not produce any money. Then, rather than fess up and admit my theft attempt, I lied again and said I had mistakenly left my money at home and if he would just allow me about fifteen minutes, I would go home and quickly return to pay for the snacks.

Recognizing that such a bungled attempt had to be the work of someone not accustomed to stealing, and wanting to teach me a lesson, the store manager decided to play along a bit more. He threatened to call the police unless I called my parents to come to the store to pick me up. With little choice, I entered a phone booth knowing full well that if I called my parents, Dad would likely arrive with belt in hand, which at the time seemed worse than serving jail time. Nevertheless, I entered the phone booth and realized I did not have the ten cents required to make the call.

So I closed the phone booth door, pretended to drop a dime in the coin slot, and moved my lips as though I was having a conversation. I then emerged from the phone booth and announced my parents were at work and could not come to the store.

At this point, my accomplices were literally on the floor laughing, and one even yelled out, "You know your mother does not work!" The store manager seemed agitated as he reminded me that when making a phone call, he could hear the dime being inserted into the coin slot, but for some reason he did not hear anything this time. At that point, I was on the verge of a breakdown and full-throated confession, when the store manager told me to go home and not return. As you can imagine, my friends teased me all the way home. The good news is I never attempted to steal anything ever again.

Addiction

There was another subtle consequence of my lack of academic performance and low self-esteem: I started to overeat. This was not a conscious or deliberate decision; instead it was gradual. The fact that my parents insisted we clean our plates during every meal did not help. Plus the reward I looked forward to after forcing down brussels sprouts and broccoli was dessert. If there was not a homemade cake or pie around, the kitchen cabinets were always filled with sweet snacks. Pop Tarts, Little Debbie snacks, and bags of cookies became my constant companion. As a special treat, our parents would visit a local ice cream shop or one of our favorites, McDonald's.

Food became a refuge from the challenges of growing up on the Horseshoe. Unfortunately, the more overweight I became, the more the neighborhood kids teased me. Even worse than the verbal jabs from the neighborhood kids, the fact that some of those closest to me were embarrassed by my weight really hurt. At home, I was constantly harassed about what I ate, how much I ate, and that I should be on a diet. I justified the excess weight as necessary for entry into the NFL. I carefully tracked height and weight statistics of my favorite NFL players because I wanted to look like them. Only in hindsight did I realize my overeating was driven by my poor self-esteem and not my dreams of NFL stardom.

Deep down, I think I knew overeating was bad for my health. But as a preteen, what was likely meant as constructive advice sounded demeaning and more like deep, piercing insults. The experience of being overweight as a kid was so impactful that today I am very health-conscious. I rarely miss a day of exercise, and I try hard to eat a healthy diet. Because of my childhood experience with food, I empathize with those struggling with weight because I experienced the name calling and stereotypes of being lazy and gluttonous. I also empathize with those struggling with other addictions because overeating is an addiction. And like other addictions, maintaining a healthy weight can be a lifelong struggle.

The 1960s Culture and Colored Television

Prior to the civil rights awakening in the late 1960s and early 1970s, adults on the Horseshoe reflected the attitudes and lack of self-esteem of the times. The "conk" hairstyle was popular and worn by many of the adult men in the neighborhood. The term "conk" refers to the hair product congolene, a gel used to "straighten" one's hair. In the Spike Lee movie *Malcolm X*, there is a memorable scene where young Malcolm X, played by Denzel Washington, panicked when the application of congolene, which included lye, became unbearably hot to his scalp when he could not find a water source to wash it out. Celebrities like James Brown, Chuck Berry, and Little Richard helped popularize the hairstyle. During the civil rights movement, conk hairstyles became taboo, as they were viewed as black men trying to look "white" and being ashamed of their natural hair.

"Colored" actors rarely appeared on television, and when they did it was the talk of the neighborhood, even though many played subservient roles, or pimps and crooks. Oprah Winfrey recounted this same experience during her youth, as the mere sighting of an African American on television was occasion to alert all the neighbors. Winfrey said, "We would call them to say, 'Colored people are on TV! Colored people are on!'" Winfrey recalled that the only black "role model" she remembered viewing on TV was the character Buckwheat on the *Little Rascals* comedy series.[3]

Reading that story hit home because on the Horseshoe, the neighborhood call of "Colored people are on TV!" was a common refrain. My siblings and I religiously watched the *Little Rascals* on television, and, like Winfrey, our favorite character was Buckwheat. Although we thought the character was hilarious at the time, Buckwheat spoke broken English and frequently got into mischief. What we did not understand at the time was that the image of Buckwheat helped form our own images and unfortunately also painted a stereotype of black Americans for white Americans.

My earliest recollection of "colored TV" is a program my parents watched called *Amos 'n' Andy*. In the story line, Amos Jones and Andy Brown worked on a farm near Atlanta, Georgia, and during the first week's episodes, they moved to Chicago for a better life. They made the trip with four ham-and-cheese sandwiches and $24. Once in Chicago, they lived in a rooming house and eventually started their own business, the Fresh Air Taxi Company. The pair was often joined by George "Kingfish" Stevens, who was known for his get-rich-quick schemes. Kingfish made the catchphrase "Holy mackerel" part of household lexicon. I remember how my parents and relatives laughed at the comedic characters on the show. Despite its popularity, though, the show depicted a subservient view of black family life that generated a fair amount of controversy.

While these and other television shows like them provided opportunities for black actors and actresses to secure acting roles, I don't think anyone could have predicted the negative stereotypes that would result. Likewise, witnessing adult men go to such lengths to alter their natural hairstyle was confusing for me. In those days, an African American born with a light complexion and curly hair was still deemed to have "good hair," and was thus considered more desirable or physically attractive. Even as a youngster this made little sense to me. I vividly recall the feelings of inferiority and internal struggle with a society that, at best, referred to me as a minority. Unknown at the time was the impact these stereotypes would have on my personal self-esteem well into my adult years.

Be an Ant, Not a Grasshopper

In third grade, I had no idea how much of an impact my teacher would have on my life as she read aloud to the class one of Aesop's Fables: "The Ant and the Grasshopper." The story chronicled a happy-go-lucky grasshopper who spent his summer having fun and playing his violin. While enjoying the last of the warm weather in the fall, the grasshopper noticed a family of ants, busily scurrying about stockpiling food for the coming winter. The grasshopper tried to encourage the ants to slow down and enjoy themselves, but the ants were determined to gather food stocks while they could so they would be prepared for winter. When winter arrived, a thick blanket of snow made it impossible for the grasshopper to find food, yet the family of ants was comfortable in their home with plenty of food to eat.

This story of frugality and saving had a profound impact on both my personal and professional lives. In addition to this children's story, perhaps the largest influencer that birthed my passion for cost savings and hard work was Dad. Every day I watched him leave home at 5:00 a.m. and return late. During his free time, he serviced his own car, fixed our plumbing and carpentry, and bought items in bulk to save money. To save on groceries he raised a large garden until he was well into his seventies. Fishing and hunting were as much about putting food on the table as they were about recreation. Dad constructed a brick chimney and installed a wood stove in our basement to cut down on heating costs. While doing so, he cut a hole in the basement ceiling so the heat could travel up to their bedroom during cold nights.

I took mental notes as I watched this master at saving money secure wood for the stove. With his connections in the city, a phone call would lead to the two of us arriving at a city block where D.C. workers cut down large trees that were a nuisance. The on-site supervisor met Dad at the back of his truck, had a quick shot of whiskey, and exchanged $20, and the workers placed the large chunks of wood on the back of our truck. Following the transaction, Dad and I returned home, cut the large chunks into stove-size pieces, and stacked them in the backyard until winter.

My first method of earning money was cutting grass and washing cars for the neighbors on the Horseshoe. My most reliable customer was our adjoining duplex neighbor, Mr. Nathaniel Hines. Mr. Hines was a kind gentleman who was married with two daughters and who worked for the State Department. We could hear much of what went on in his household through the paper-thin walls that separated us. I often winced when my parents argued because I assumed his family could hear them as well. When the school year ended in summer of 1963, I, then ten years old, knocked on his door.

"Hello, Larry," he greeted me. "What are you up to this summer?"

I responded, "Good morning, Mr. Hines. I really need to earn some money and I was wondering if you might let me cut your grass and maybe wash and wax your car."

Mr. Hines thought for a moment and said, "When you say cut the grass, does that include trimming around the edges?"

"Of course," I responded. "I'll do a really good job and I'll shine your car up really nice also."

"Okay," he said, "how much?"

This question caught me quite by surprise. I had rehearsed my speech to get the job, but I had no idea how much to charge. This was long before weed eaters were invented, so trimming his yard meant using hand-held manual clippers, on my hands and knees, clipping grass along the edges of his large yard.

I estimated the job would take about two hours, so, without any cost-estimating experience, I said, "How does two dollars sound?" Recognizing he was getting the deal of the century, he maintained a poker face and said, "Sounds good. How about two dollars to wash and wax the car as well?"

"Yes, sir," I responded, "and thank you, I'll get started on your car right away."

During the winter, I walked the Horseshoe with a shovel and earned money for shoveling snow from the front steps, walkway, and sidewalk. I maintained my $2.00 charge, and for reasons unknown at the time, no one argued with my price! Dad opened a bank account for me, and it gave me great pleasure to watch my account accumulate, with interest, at $2.00 individual deposits. Although I was generally a poor student in school, those lessons on the theory of compound interest were forever etched in my brain.

Later I expanded my work portfolio as a delivery boy for the *Washington Post* newspaper and the now-defunct *Washington Daily News*. The arrangement was that I would deliver the papers to an address list provided by the newspaper, collect the fee from the customers, and pay the newspaper their share. The surplus was my salary. Unfortunately, this venture did not work out because collecting newspaper fees from subsidized housing project customers was not only difficult, but I also got cursed out several times for simply knocking on their doors and repeating my biweekly message, "Collect for the Post." Though my objective was to make money, not lose money, I ended my career delivering newspapers owing the newspaper company money.

At twelve years old I decided to be an entrepreneur by opening my own lemonade stand. I figured if someone can drive around in a truck playing music and sell ice cream, I could be successful selling a thirst-quenching beverage. On a warm day, I made two pitchers of lemonade, placed them in my toy wagon, borrowed paper cups from Mom, and set up in front of our home for business. The initial response from the neighborhood kids was laughter and teasing. But with a price point of 10 cents per cup, before long I was back and forth in our kitchen, making more lemonade to satisfy a rapidly growing demand.

As I glanced into the pork and beans can that I used to collect money and make change, I was quite proud of myself. I even fantasized about expanding my business to include chips and other snacks and calling it "Larry's Snack Wagon." My dream bubble was popped, however, when an older kid on the block with a reputation for being tough asked to see how much money was in my can, and promptly walked away with all my money. This was my first day in the food sales business, and I was robbed. I desperately wanted to tell my parents or, worse, tell the perpetrator's parents. Knowing that either course of action would surely result in a personal pummeling, though, I thought better of it.

Are Coloreds Allowed?

At the age of ten I ran into the house with some news. There was a new movie theater about to open just up the street from the Horseshoe. I had never been to a movie theater before and was anxious to do so. I specifically asked Mom to take me to see the movie *Ben Hur*, starring Charlton Heston. All the neighborhood kids were talking about the movie, and I was excited to see it. I'll never forget the picture of uncertainty on Mom's face when I broke the news. Without revealing her concern to me, it was not clear to her if blacks would be allowed to attend the new theater. Instead of answering me directly, she responded, "I'll see."

I then watched her go into the kitchen and pick up the phone. As I secretly listened, she called the theater. Using her best white voice, Mom asked if colored people were allowed in the theater. Based on a conversation she had with Dad later that evening, I surmised that the person answering her telephone call replied that indeed colored people were allowed in the theater if they dressed nicely and behaved themselves. Whereas today I would consider that an insulting response, Mom was not at all offended, and she and I attended the movie theater the following weekend. And, yes, we dressed nicely and behaved ourselves.

Despite my challenges with daily life on the Horseshoe, I did have an annual respite. Most of my summers as a youth were spent on my grandfather's farm in Red House, Virginia. Those visits represented the classic love-hate relationship. While I detested rising each morning at the crack of dawn and working in hot and humid tobacco fields, I absolutely loved the seclusion and solace the farm offered. Each summer I transitioned from inner city to country life. Each summer, I left my friends and siblings behind to live with my grandparents. Each summer, I learned to appreciate the calm and simple life of living and working on a farm.

2
RED HOUSE

What I learned growing up on the farm was
a way of life that was centered on hard
work, and on faith and on thrift. Those values
have stuck with me my whole life.

—GOVERNOR RICK PERRY[1]

I was eleven years old and the sweltering heat was almost unbearable. My grandfather and I were working in one of several tobacco fields when I spotted what I believed to be the largest squirrel I had ever seen. This curious creature then spotted me and began running to the top of a twenty-five-foot tree. I alerted my grandfather to this activity, to which he replied, "Boy, are you kidding? That's not a squirrel, that is a groundhog." I had neither seen nor heard of a groundhog, but I was fascinated by its stature and speed. We continued about our work in the tobacco field, but the entire time I kept my eye on this creature, which dutifully remained perched on a limb at the top of the tree. An hour or so later, my grandfather said, "Larry, it's getting too hot, let's head for the house. By the way, have you ever eaten a groundhog before?"

"Absolutely not. Can you really eat those things?" We walked toward his tractor where he had a shotgun, already loaded and tucked away. He checked the shotgun, took aim, and shot at the groundhog. The groundhog remained on the limb, so I assumed my grandfather's shot had missed. But rather than take a second shot, my grandfather put the gun away and we waited. A few minutes later, the groundhog scampered to the main trunk of the tree, ran down, and fell dead on the ground at my grand-father's feet. He picked up the animal, threw it on the back of the tractor, and said, "Let's go."

We returned to the main house, and my grandfather took the groundhog to the woodpile and carefully cleaned it. He handed the cleaned carcass to me with instructions to take it to my grandmother. She was busy working in the kitchen, but she accepted the groundhog and said, "Go help your grandfather, dinner will be ready in about an hour." At the dinner table, she lifted the oval-shaped top of a steaming hot pot that revealed the now-cooked groundhog, smothered in gravy and surrounded by cooked carrots, potatoes, and onions. I reluctantly took a small helping of roasted groundhog and was surprised that it wasn't too bad. In fact, covered with gravy and all the trimmings, it tasted pretty good. But I had to be careful biting into the meat as some of the shotgun shell pellets were still embedded.

Farm Life

Some of the best time of my youth was spent on my grandparents' farm. In many ways, those visits provided a valuable contrast to life on the Horseshoe. The small town of Red House is in the southern central region of Virginia. It is roughly eleven miles south of historic Appomattox. The town of Red House was only distinguishable by a single stop sign and a corner store with a red tin roof. The topography is rolling hills, beautifully aged trees, and farmland. The mostly paved two-lane roadways had no markings or posted speed limits. I mostly visited during the 1960s, when there was a clear demarcation between blacks and whites. I never noticed any facilities or establishments that were off-limits to blacks, but we were strictly taught to be on our best behavior when in the presence of whites.

My grandfather, Charlie Spencer, or P.A. (pronounced "pee-ay") for short, owned a farm off the main road, down a long, winding dirt-gravel secondary road to finally a plain dirt road that disappeared into a wooded area. Once you cleared the trees, a wide expanse revealed a sprawling farm with a modest wooden home shielded with a light-brown brick pattern asphalt cover. The roof was covered with tin, which played a symphony of sleeping music when it rained at night. P.A. built the home in the 1920s, when there was no available electricity or indoor plumbing. Two large apple trees anchored the two corners of the front yard and provided an ample supply of apples for pies and fried for breakfast. Centered between the two apple trees was a manual water pump that supplied water for drinking, bathing, and cooking.

P.A. was born in 1898, the grandson of a slave. He served overseas in the U.S. Army during World War I. He returned from the war and became a schoolteacher. Surprisingly, none of his offspring conclusively knew how and where he was educated. What is verifiable is he was frequently called upon to read and interpret important papers for illiterate neighbors and friends. P.A. purchased sixty-three acres of farmland in three tranches: A portion was purchased from my grandmother's family and the remaining was acquired from two adjoining landowners. During the 1920s and 1930s, a colored man owning his own farm was highly prized and represented a significant step forward from sharecropping. As was the custom of the time, he was clearly the "man" and disciplinarian of the family. His word was final. There was no back talk or questioning his judgment or authority.

My grandmother, Francis, or M.A. (pronounced "em-ay") for short, was born in 1908. My grandparents met when P.A. boarded with M.A.'s family and was her schoolteacher. Whereas P.A. displayed a gruff and stoic exterior, M.A. was the opposite. She was the epitome of perpetual motion, always wore a smile, and had an infectious laugh. She rose each morning before the crow of the rooster and worked nonstop until bedtime. I awoke each morning to the smell of fresh eggs, home-cured bacon, and homemade biscuits, all prepared from scratch on a wood-burning stove. She fed the chickens, cats, and dogs, cleaned the house, hand-washed clothes, and hung them to dry on a makeshift outdoor clothesline. I watched her milk the cow, churn butter, and make delicious cakes and pies.

My grandparents had nine children, four boys and five girls. The one thing they had in common was leaving the farm soon after they graduated from high school. For the most part, the girls went on to achieve higher education, either in teaching or nursing, which at the time were the only alternatives for young black women. The boys, however, all entered the military. My first full summer visit to the farm was at age ten. It was the summer that their youngest offspring, my Uncle Tony, was about to make his escape from the farm into the military. It was around noon when the dogs started barking, alerting us of an approaching vehicle. I looked up the road and saw a car approaching, leaving a trail of dust from the dry dirt road.

I had never seen an official government vehicle before, and I was certainly not prepared for the gentleman who exited the car. My grandparents went to greet our visitor, a sharp-looking U.S. Marine. I noted the sharp crease in his pants and the high shine on his shoes. I moved closer to listen in on the conversation and heard the Marine say, "All he'll need is a change of underwear for one night. We'll take care of the rest." A minute or two later, Uncle Tony emerged from the house with a small bag of clothes and entered the vehicle. He didn't say a word to me or to his parents. I could only assume that they had said their goodbyes inside the house. Nevertheless, the Marine and Uncle Tony headed back up the dusty road, and it would be several years before I would see him again.

A distinct advantage of my summer visits was that my grandparents were raising my cousin Bernard Spencer. Bernard's mother, my Aunt Phyllis, lived in Philadelphia. With the nearest home about a half-mile away, Bernard looked forward to my visits because aside from attending school, he was completely isolated year-round with our grandparents. P.A. owned a small black-and-white TV that we rarely watched, unless one of his two favorite shows, *Lassie* or *Bonanza*, was playing. Our geographic location was so remote I could not connect with a signal to listen to "soul" music on my transistor radio. Aside from attending church on Sunday, we seldom left the confines of the farm.

Chickens freely roamed through the yard while hunting dogs slept in the summer shade. Fields of corn and rows of tobacco stretched as far as the eye could see. Hundreds of colorful butterflies fluttered from flower to flower, and hummingbirds suspended themselves in midair to sample the nectar from M.A.'s flower gardens. We gathered fresh eggs early each morning from the makeshift chicken coop. There was a single cow named "Bossy," whose cowbell clanged back and forth as she grazed in the lush green pasture. Her pasture mate, "Kate," was a large farm horse that never flinched when P.A. hitched her to various types of farm equipment to pull.

Both animals were housed in a barn constructed with logs and wood, where dirt daubers built their nests in the red mud cementing the log joints. Just east of the house was an old-fashioned woodshed with an overhead structure where P.A. parked his green 1950 Chevrolet Bel Air. Just south of the house was an old smokehouse where cured meat hung with brown twine and homemade preserved fruits and vegetables lined the wooden shelves.

Rounding out the immediate structures adjacent to the home was a smaller barn for grain and corn with an overhang for the tractor and farm truck and an adjacent hog pen. I particularly enjoyed the covered back porch on the main house that had a panoramic view of the beautiful farm fields and a distant barn where I could hear the call of the whippoorwills in the trees. Also, however, the back porch offered a direct view of the dreaded outhouse, which was my least favorite structure on the farm.

Farm life was the antithesis of life on the Horseshoe. Rather than sleep in during the summer, P.A. had the entire house up and ready for work at the crack of dawn. My first job each morning was to feed or slop the hogs. It was all I could handle to carry the two large buckets of what we called "slop"—a concoction of table scraps, a powdery substance for nutrition, and water—across the yard to the hog pen. As though they had a sixth sense, the hogs began grunting and snorting as I approached the pen, and I could hardly pour the slop into the trough as they crowded in to get their share.

Most of our daily food was produced on the farm. Vegetable gardens were plentiful, and we picked wild blackberries from bushes in the woods for M.A.'s famous cobbler. Meat was also produced on the farm. The annual slaughtering of the hogs and an occasional cow, while it produced a lot of meat, was not something I enjoyed watching. Whenever we spotted M.A. wielding an ax, we knew chicken was on the menu for dinner. She very calmly walked into the front yard, grabbed a chicken by the feet, walked down to the woodpile, and chopped off its head. She then released the chicken as it literally ran around like a chicken with its head cut off. In addition to my culinary introduction to roasted groundhog, we also occasionally dined on rabbits and squirrels.

I'm told that a rooster has an internal clock that causes it to crow just before the sun comes up, so each morning I awoke to the screeching call of our rooster. My grandmother apparently had an internal clock of her own because the smell of her home-cooked breakfast was already in the air. Following a hearty breakfast, P.A., Bernard, and I boarded the tractor and traveled to one of several tobacco fields. Our routine was to walk through each planted row and "top" the tobacco plants and pull "suckers." Topping and suckering tobacco plants is necessary for healthy, high-producing plants. Topping is manually breaking off a flowery growth on the top of the plant, while suckering is manually removing small leaf-like growths, called suckers, at the base of the stalk of each leaf. I had no idea at the time about the poor health effects of the thick brown tar that accumulated on my arms and hands as we walked through the rows of five-foot-tall tobacco plants. A side benefit was collecting the green tobacco worms in our pockets, which were akin to caterpillars, that we used for fishing bait.

As soon as work for the day was done, Bernard and I would engage in our favorite pastime: fishing. Actually, it was our only pastime. Fishing was typically done in one of several small ponds or creeks on the farm. In addition to tobacco worms, Bernard and I spent hours catching grasshoppers, digging earthworms, and scrounging other insects for bait. Our fishing equipment was primitive and consisted of a tree branch with fishing line and a hook and bobber attached. During a creative moment, I designed and built a fish net to catch minnows for bait. The net was built with tobacco sticks, which were used to hang the tobacco for curing, and a used burlap sack.

Growing up on the Horseshoe, I was not accustomed to removing my shoes and wading into a creek with who knows what on the bottom, so I offered Bernard the chance to test out our new design. Together we found a great spot in the curve of a creek in the cow pasture of a neighbor. Bernard removed his shoes, rolled up his pants legs, and waded into the dark water. On the very first try, he scooped up a net full of small minnows and crawfish. We were overjoyed by this success, so I collected the minnows and crawfish in a small bucket, and Bernard waded in again. This time, as he poked and prodded the sticks and burlap under the shallow bank, a water moccasin struck out from under the bank directly at Bernard. Fortunately, the snake did not make contact, but Bernard and I likely set a world record running back to the house, leaving the net and fishing equipment behind.

As the old saying goes, every Saturday evening, Bernard and I took a bath whether we needed one or not. Since there was no indoor plumbing, we used an aluminum water tub with handles on each end and filled it from the manual water pump in the front yard. We flipped a coin to determine who bathed in the cold water first because we only pumped water into the tub one time. I never gave a second thought to bathing completely naked in the front yard because no one was around to see. But with the abundance of dirt we both accumulated during the week of working in the fields, in hindsight I would have opted to refill the tub rather than bathe in used bath water.

I often felt bad for Bernard. His mother lived hundreds of miles away, he had no contact with or knowledge of his biological father, and P.A. was a strict disciplinarian. Because I wasn't a permanent resident on the farm, P.A. mostly spared the rod with me. Unfortunately, that was not the case for Bernard, whom he often beat with a switch for infractions that seemed minor. One of Bernard's few pleasures was listening to his beloved Philadelphia Phillies play baseball on a small transistor radio, alone in his room.

I often wondered if he could simply come back to D.C. and live with us. Bringing another teenager into an already overcrowded house, though, was out of the question. Many years later, I asked Bernard how he felt about being raised by our grandparents. His response was, "At the time it was the only life I knew. I worked my butt off, and I was confused about the situation with Mom but there wasn't really much I could do about it." Bernard graduated from high school in June 1971. Less than a month later, like his uncles before him, Bernard left our grandparents' home for the last time to join the U.S. military.

My Spiritual Reckoning

Faith is a large part of the African American experience, and my siblings and I were raised in a Christian home, so church on Sunday was mandatory. Back home we attended the Tabernacle Baptist Church on Division Avenue in southeast D.C. Mom was an usher and Dad served as a trustee of the church. Predominantly black Baptist churches are known for lengthy services, but Tabernacle offered a separate youth service in the basement that was better-suited for our spiritual development and attention span. Sitting directly beneath the adult parishioners, we could hear the rhythmic tapping of shoes through the ceiling as the gospel music stirred the souls of the congregation. We also overheard the occasional heightened enunciation of the pastor preaching the Word, followed by a chorus of "amen" and "take your time."

On the farm, since P.A. was a church deacon, attending church on Sundays was nonnegotiable. We attended the Mount Zion Baptist Church in Red House. It was a small church with an upper balcony. There was no paved parking and the paint was chipped on the wood-slatted exterior. There was no air conditioning and the summers were warm and humid, so the hand-held fans with a picture of Martin Luther King Jr. on one side and a funeral home advertisement on the other were literally in full swing. There was a shortage of pastors at the time, so most clergyman pastored several churches. In the case of the Mount Zion church, "preaching" was only one Sunday each month, while the remaining Sundays consisted of Sunday school and Bible study.

Revival is a special annual, weeklong church event where a guest minister is invited and preaching is held each evening. The purpose of revival service is to inspire the church congregation and gain new converts. In the tradition of the black church, which dates to slavery, revival services are filled with emotion and passion. At age fourteen, I was sitting in the upper balcony of Mount Zion Church during revival as the minister began his sermon. Like never before, I was focused on his every word. It was as though he was preaching just to me. At the end of the service, I felt the power of God pulling me to get up from my pew, walk down the aisle to the front of the church, and commit my life to Christ and be baptized. In the Baptist tradition, being baptized meant having the pastor fully submerge me.

For the time being I resisted that "call" but felt a little ashamed as I watched my cousin Bernard make the journey forward. Later that summer, P.A. took me to a revival service at a neighboring St. Andrews Baptist Church, where a cousin on my mother's side of the family, Vinston Goldman, attended. The personal call I previously felt still lingered, but this time it was too strong to resist, so at the end of preaching, I made my journey down the church aisle. Unlike Mount Zion Church, St. Andrews did not have an indoor baptismal pool; instead they had an outdoor pool that resembled a cinder block bathtub. There was a manual water pump at the front of the pool that had previously filled the structure with water.

The night of my baptism was warm and humid, and I was really nervous. As instructed, I was dressed in a pair of shorts and T-shirt. The congregation gathered outside around the pool and began singing spiritual hymns. As I stepped down into the cool water and took my place beside the preacher, he said, "I now baptize you in the name of the Father, the Son, and the Holy Spirit." He then leaned me back into the water until I was completely submerged and quickly brought me back upright. I'm not sure why but the first face I saw as I emerged from the water was that of my cousin Laverne Goldman. As I stood there, dripping water and standing under the stars, I was no longer nervous. In fact, I experienced a sense of calm that night that is beyond explanation or description.

As P.A. drove Bernard and me home that night, I pondered what had just occurred. I had been taught not to lie or cheat or steal, and I generally tried to be a good person. But that experience helped me understand that there is a larger force in our lives. I understood that no matter what happened in my life, God would be there to guide and protect me. The call I felt during revival was real. Sure, the service was emotional, but it was not emotion that caused me to walk down the aisle of a standing-room-only church service that night. It was God, and it forever changed my life. That's not to say I became a perfect person and exhibited flawless behavior and character—not by a long shot. But it instilled in me a formidable force that has guided me to seek to be a better person.

A Life Lesson

My last full-summer visit to the farm was at age fifteen, where I experienced yet another life-transforming event. When I arrived at P.A.'s farm, I was surprised to discover my cousin Bernard was not there. He had traveled to Philadelphia to visit with his mother. Bernard would join me a couple of weeks later, but I was not aware of that arrangement beforehand. Since P.A. generally viewed me as a lazy city kid and of not much "account," I suspected that he was not happy with me. But this summer was different. With just the two of us, he suddenly took great interest in my development and began "mentoring" me on the ways of the world, at least the world as he knew it. For example, I was never particularly interested in the difference between a mule and a donkey, but he thought that was one of those golden nuggets of wisdom I needed to know. He also said, "Even a blind rooster finds a kernel of corn every once in a while." I'm still scratching my head over that one.

To reciprocate, I really did try to work a little harder to show him what I was made of. Early one morning we skipped working the tobacco fields, and instead P.A. hitched up the horse and we headed for a patch of land about a mile from the house. When we arrived, he positioned himself behind a plow and proceeded to plow perfect rows in the newly turned soil. Plowing a field behind a horse is not something you see growing up in D.C., so I was fixated on him as he and the horse manipulated the plow, in unison, up and down the field. After about thirty minutes, P.A. stopped to take a "potty" break in the woods, and I was left to wait for his return.

As P.A. disappeared into the woods, I got the bright idea that I could really impress him if I continued his work until he returned. So, with no clue about how to plow a field, I positioned myself behind the horse and gave the command, "come up," which cued the horse to walk forward. The horse and I hadn't taken two steps when I realized plowing a field was much harder than it looked. There is a special skill required to maneuver a plow and stay in rhythm with the horse, and needless to say I did not possess that skill. After a few more steps I realized two things: first, I was cutting across my grandfather's perfectly plowed rows, and second, I knew how to get the horse to move forward but I had no idea how to make the horse stop.

So there we were, the horse smartly cutting diagonally across the field and me literally running behind to keep up. After what seemed like hours, P.A. emerged from the woods and in total disbelief, he yelled out, "Larry, what are you doing?!" When I heard his voice I simultaneously panicked and stumbled. During my stumble, to balance myself, I instinctively yelled, "Whoa!" Much to my surprise the horse stopped! This was quite a relief but it was short-lived because before I had a chance to survey the damage, I noticed my grandfather storming across the field toward me. Immediately I was gripped with fear as I looked around to the adjacent woods and saw the myriad potential "switches," which was the disciplinary tool of choice on the farm.

Of course, today, physically striking a child for disciplinary purposes is mostly discouraged and, depending on the severity, could be illegal. But that was not the case in the 1960s. In fact, whipping or spanking children was not only permissible but also encouraged. Besides, who would even know what took place on a farm in the middle of nowhere?

When he caught up to me, he first asked if I was all right; that was the first surprise. He then explained why the fine art of plowing behind a horse is typically reserved for those with proper experience, not to mention strength. With my mind still fixated on the young firm dogwood tree limbs within arm's reach, my grandfather said something that has guided me my entire life. In surprise number two, his simple and perhaps inarticulate words were, "It's okay to try and fail but it's not okay not to try." Without saying it, in his own way he was proud that I had tried. From that day forward, our relationship was very different. On that day and in that instant, I was not a city kid, but I was his grandson who was trying his best to impress his grandfather.

My relationship with P.A. was complex. I respected him for what he accomplished in his life during the Jim Crow era. As individuals, however, we could not have been more dissimilar. We were essentially from two different worlds and certainly two different generations. He was not accustomed to being challenged, especially by a teenager, but I occasionally pushed back on him, which irritated him to no end. A few days following the field-plowing episode, P.A. and I were back in the tobacco fields when I noticed M.A. making her way toward us. M.A. did not drive but the roughly two-mile walk did not appear to faze her. She found P.A. and me covered with tobacco tar, and they had a brief conversation. P.A. motioned to me to get on the tractor, and we headed back to the house.

When we arrived home, P.A. and I washed off the tobacco tar, went directly to his car, and headed up the dusty road toward the main highway that would take us to the city of Appomattox, Virginia. I had no idea why we were traveling to Appomattox, so, as was my normal posture, I just sat quietly. As we entered the small country town, I looked outside my car window when suddenly I saw my cousin Bernard and Aunt Phyllis standing alongside the street. In my excitement,

I yelled out to my grandfather, "P.A., there is Bernard and Phyllis!" I was shocked to hear my grandfather's immediate and direct rebuke to shut up and be quiet. I was confused by his reaction but said nothing as he made a U-turn and picked up my cousin and aunt.

Once we were on our way back home and had cleared the city limits, P.A. turned to me and said, "Don't you ever yell or raise your voice when white people are around again. Don't you know they will grab you and beat you for raising your voice like that?" Growing up in D.C., I had never heard that before. I had clearly noted, however, that both my parents seemed uneasy around whites and even altered their diction when in their presence. But it had not occurred to me they had been raised to fear whites. When we returned home, I pulled my cousin Bernard aside and asked what P.A.'s comment was about. Surprisingly, Bernard agreed with P.A.'s reaction and cautioned me to be careful around "white folks."

The contrast of inner-city living with the serene and picturesque farm helped shape the person I would become. Standing on the back porch of P.A.'s home and looking over the vast expanse of rolling farmland created a sense of awe and peace associated with the beauty of our planet that I continuously long for. It was a simple life and a simple scene, but the sense of calm and tranquility I experienced there has lasted a lifetime. Often during a stressful time, I close my eyes, breathe deeply, and with my mind's eye I find myself once again on P.A.'s back porch. I can feel the warmth of the summer air, hear the chickens pecking at the ground in the yard, and I can see a tattered barn off in the distance.

The work ethic displayed by my grandparents is certainly something that was etched into my being. My experience with their church revival provided a spiritual foundation that will forever guide my life. Watching M.A. toil and work gave me an indelible example of a strong woman that shaped my appreciation and respect for women in my life and in our society. Perhaps above all, my gruff and oftentimes overly strict grandfather showed me the face of a black man who, despite living in the era of Jim Crow, worked hard every day to support his church, his family, and himself.

3

FISH OUT OF WATER

Being a fish out of water is tough,
but that's how you evolve.

—KUMAIL NANJIANI[1]

In 1966, midway through eighth grade in junior high school, Dad retired from the Army after twenty-two years. So it was no surprise to see him when I arrived home from school. It was unusual, though, to see him on a ladder spackling over cracks in the ceiling. As I headed upstairs to change clothes, I joked with Dad that he must really be bored to repair ceiling cracks that had existed for years. As I disappeared to the second floor, he yelled, "Don't plan on spending much time playing outside today. I need you to help me prepare the house for sale."

I froze in my tracks and carefully backed down the steps and asked, "What do you mean? Are we moving?"

"Yes," he responded. "Hurry up and change clothes because some people are coming over to look at the house tomorrow."

After retirement, Dad accepted a civil service job as a photographer at Fort Detrick, Maryland. My parents never discussed their finances or personal business with us, but this was an exception. I was quite surprised to learn we would be moving to Seat Pleasant, Maryland, a suburban community just a few miles across the D.C. border. It was the dream and a mark of success for black families to move from the inner city to the suburbs. The home was a two-story split-level with a modest-sized yard. The purchase price was $21,900. My siblings would attend an elementary school that was a short walk from our house. But I, as a junior high school student, would ride the school bus. Almost as an aside, Dad mentioned that our new home was in an all-white neighborhood.

That revelation caused high anxiety in me, not because I had anything against moving to a white neighborhood, but because the Horseshoe was all I knew. It was my comfort zone, and it was 100 percent black. Up to that point in my life, my friends, my church, and my schoolmates were all black. I wondered if the new neighbors would accept us. Would they call us names? Would I be able to make new friends? What about school? How would the teachers treat me? Would the football team accept me? I felt like a fish out of water as these questions and more invaded my mind as I watched the moving crew pack our belongings and load the eighteen-wheel moving truck.

As we drove down the street of our new home for the first time, neighbors peeked through their curtains to see the new arrivals. As the movers began to unload the truck, Dad drove me to Pullen Junior High School to register. I didn't say a word as he spoke with the school counselor and arranged my schedule to begin the following day. My silence masked my angst about this sudden life change. I could not help but notice the stark contrasts from the school I had just left. Compared to Sousa Junior High, the building was clean and the outside grounds were well groomed. Unlike the more chaotic experience I left behind, students moved briskly and orderly through the hallways between classes.

Pullen's student body and faculty were about 50 percent black, so I said to myself that assimilating into this new environment might not be so difficult. On the other hand, Pullen had a reputation as a tough school because many of the students lived in Palmer Park, Maryland, where, among others, future world champion boxer Sugar Ray Leonard resided. On the car ride back home, I started convincing myself that this move just might work out after all. Pullen had a great athletic program with great coaches, and from the short interaction I had in the school office, everyone seemed nice and welcoming. As it turned out, however, not everyone was happy at my arrival.

Confronting a Bully

The following morning, I stepped onto the orange and black school bus to see mostly white faces, many gawking at me while they whispered under their breath. The atmosphere was intimidating as I made my way through the aisle searching for a seat. There were several students sitting on the aisle side of the bench seats designed for two, but no one moved over to offer me a seat. As I made my way to the back of the bus, I noticed one of the few black kids with a scowl on his face staring at me, so I dared not say a word. It seemed like the three-mile bus trip to Pullen took forever. When I arrived, I received my new class schedule and made my way to class. As I entered civics class, that same black kid with the brash look on his face was sitting in the back of the class with his eyes trained on my every move.

I tried my best to ignore him until finally I had enough. Rather than be confrontational, I simply greeted him and introduced myself. He responded, "I don't talk to punks like you and after class I'm going to kick your ass!" This response caught me completely off guard. I hardly knew this guy and already he wanted to fight. I racked my brain as to why this kid wanted conflict with a complete stranger, and I could not understand his action. But he made the threat in front of the entire class, and once again I was backed into a corner of either fighting or facing the ridicule of backing down.

The bus ride home that afternoon was agonizing. The entire bus was buzzing about the impending fight, and this kid stared me down the entire time. I considered asking the school bus driver to intervene, but that would have made me look weak. At that point, I figured I had no choice but to fight this guy. I exited the bus before he did and someone in the gathering crowd offered to hold my books. My opponent then exited the bus, put up his hands, and said, "Let's go, punk. You D.C. guys think you're tough. I'll show you who's tough."

He was taller, but I was much stockier and stronger. He swung at me and missed, and I countered and connected with his jaw. The punch backed him up, and I was on him before he could collect himself. The crowd was roaring and my adrenalin was pumping as I continued to punch him without any return fire. Finally, he surrendered by saying, "Enough," and he picked up his books and walked away. The crowd congratulated me for beating up a neighborhood bully, but I did not feel like a hero. Truth be told, I didn't want to fight. I just wanted to go home. The silver lining of that experience was that no one bothered me for the remainder of my junior high school years.

Friendly Competition

As we settled in to the new neighborhood, I began to make friends. In particular I met Carlos Rodriquez, whose family came from Puerto Rico. He introduced himself as the best athlete on the block, to which I responded, "Says who?" Carlos and I became friends, but his quest to beat me in athletics became an obsession. We competed in everything. From a contest to determine who could throw a football the farthest to one-on-one basketball games to foot races down the middle of the street, our heated competitions became the talk of the street. Even though I liked Carlos personally, I was even more competitive than he was and was determined to beat him in every sport.

This competition ended abruptly during a basketball showdown game in the dead of winter. Carlos challenged me to a basketball game where the winner would be declared the best athlete on the block. When the contest day arrived, there were several inches of snow on the ground, so we shoveled off enough surface space to accommodate the game and got started. The agreement was a game to ten points, where whoever scored kept the ball. After twenty minutes or so, I was ahead 9 to 0 and Carlos was hopping mad. He tried everything he could to stop me from scoring that last basket, but my height and size advantage were too much for him.

As I scored the final basket, I felt bad for Carlos. He had defeated so many others on the block to claim his title but now his reign was over. Although I am a fierce competitor, I thought our battles for a meaningless title were silly. Sports were second nature to me, so I had nothing to prove to him or anyone else. Carlos and I remained friendly after that, but things were never quite the same. Within six months, Carlos and his family relocated to a different neighborhood. Within a year, our all-white neighborhood was all black.

Civil Rights Awakening

On April 4, 1968, I arrived home from school to see Mom glued to our black-and-white television. It was apparent that she was upset, but she didn't say a word. As I started downstairs to change clothes, she told me that Martin Luther King Jr. had been assassinated. She went on to say that downtown D.C. was on fire and people were looting and rioting throughout the city, and that given the events that had just occurred, I should stay in the house until things calmed down. I was quite aware of Dr. King and confused and disappointed that someone would assassinate a fellow American that was accomplishing such great things for our country.

Mom explained that although we believed Dr. King was an American icon and civil rights champion, others in our society did not agree with his agenda. She then told me that as black people, we had a long way to go to achieve the rights guaranteed by the U.S. Constitution and that we should never be intimidated or give up on our rights for equality and fair treatment. This conversation is etched in my mind because I had never heard my mother talk that way before. For years, although I knew it wasn't her fault, I resented her early lack of formal education and inability to assist with my schoolwork. That conversation, however, showed me that there was more depth to her than I understood, and that I had badly underestimated her insight. It would be years later before I completely understood why she was so versed on civil rights issues.

Unfortunately, Mom and I had a similar conversation about two months later when on June 6 of that year, Robert F. (Bobby) Kennedy was also assassinated. This time, I found Mom crying. She was distraught over his death. She explained to me that both Robert and his brother John represented hope for the black race. On June 11, 1963, President John F. Kennedy, at great political risk, had delivered an inspiring speech on civil rights that greatly stirred my parents and relatives. Mom had great admiration for both Kennedys and thought the younger brother would pick up the mantle of equality. Unfortunately, now they both had been murdered.

From that day, June 6, 1968, I committed myself to study and understand the hardships, sacrifices, and accomplishments of blacks in our history, facts I was not taught in school. By doing so, I came to admire people like Congressman John Lewis, who endured great mental and physical suffering to advance the cause of civil rights and the right to vote. As a lover of football, I read with great interest the story of famed football coach Vince Lombardi and the bigotry he and his family endured as Italian Americans. I was amazed by great black inventors like Garrett Morgan, who invented the gas mask, and Lewis Latimer, who invented the carbon filament inside of Thomas Edison's light bulb. I was delighted to learn that a black man, George Crum, even invented potato chips.

This discovery provided insight that every race and ethnicity has contributed mightily to our great nation. Growing up on the Horseshoe, though, meant I was effectively segregated. Our nation's schools were legally desegregated in 1954, but day-to-day life remained mostly segregated. That meant all my friends were black, my schoolteachers were black, my sports heroes were black, and my church congregation was black. Conversely, when I ventured outside the Horseshoe, those representing success were white. When my father bought a car, the salesman was white.

My doctor and dentist were white. Those working in local banks and large department stores were white. Even Santa Claus and my favorite superhero, Superman, were white!

This self-study helped put my life into perspective. I began to understand why my self-esteem was so poor and how that poor self-worth contributed to my poor performance in school. It also helped me understand that achieving fairness and civil rights in our country involved struggle. I somehow knew that life's playing field was tilted against blacks, but these conversations fueled a passion deep inside of me to do whatever I could to help tilt the scale back toward even.

Getting Paid

At age seventeen, I found myself holding on for dear life on the back of a garbage truck as we sped through a well-to-do neighborhood. When an uncle of a school friend offered me $20.00 per day to collect trash, I jumped at the chance. The smell was horrific and the work was hard, but I actually enjoyed the job. During the school year, I met the truck driver at 6:00 a.m. on Saturdays and picked up trash until 6:00 p.m. A side benefit was that lifting the large trash containers filled to the brim was a great physical workout that helped me get ready for football.

That same year, I applied for a job as a janitor in a local department store. I was hired on the spot for minimum wage of $1.45 per hour. Several of my coworkers, who were much older than I was, complained that I worked too hard, and they encouraged me to "take it easy and not make them look bad." But I remained focused and performed as best I could. With two weeks on the job, the supervisor called me aside and said, "Larry, we have a problem. The front office sent your application back because you are seventeen years old and the minimum age for this job is eighteen." Before I could respond, he went on, "You are a great worker and I don't want to lose you so I'm going to ignore this and hope no one asks any more questions." With that, I stripped and waxed floors in the store for the entire summer and never heard another word about my age.

The summer before my high school junior year I took on my most difficult job to date. Mr. Jim Hammond was a retired Army noncommissioned officer. He and my father met while stationed together at Forest Glen in Maryland. He was a crusty old gentleman who constantly talked about his time in Vietnam and the harsh treatment he endured as a black soldier before and after desegregation of the

Army. Due to his Army training, Hammond was a whiz at construction. He could lay bricks, build home extensions, and install outdoor drainage systems. That summer Hammond needed a laborer to help complete several jobs, and Dad figured it was time for me to get a taste of real work and, as I discovered later, a really demanding boss.

Hammond had a contract to install a wooden fence around a home in an expensive neighborhood in suburban Maryland, so on a warm summer morning he picked me up in his truck at our home at 6:30 a.m. "You ready to get your hands dirty?!" he yelled as I entered the passenger side of his truck. "Yes, sir," I responded as we pulled away for the one-hour drive to the job site. About half an hour into our journey around the D.C. beltway, his truck experienced a flat tire. Hammond carefully guided the truck over to the shoulder of the busy highway and slowed to a stop. Following a pregnant pause, he said in a firm voice, "What are you waiting for? Get out and change the tire. The tools and spare are in the back of the truck."

"Yes, sir," I responded, and as vehicles whizzed by at high speeds along the heavily traveled beltway, I assembled the jack, changed the tire, and re-entered the truck, huffing and puffing from the effort. I wanted badly to ask him why he didn't lift a finger to help, but having heard his commanding voice, I thought better of it. As we continued our trip, I wondered if I had made a mistake taking this job. When we arrived at the residence, we went right to work. Hammond had a plan laid out that we meticulously followed. Despite the summer heat, we worked twelve hours straight to complete the job.

I was bone tired when we got back on the road for the trip home. During the ride, he asked me to open the glove compartment, take out a pencil and paper, and multiply 12 times 5. I had no idea why but was too afraid to ask. I quickly replied, "12 times 5 is 60."

"You sure?" he responded, and I said, "Yes, sir." He then said, "Pull out that large envelope in the glove compartment and count out $60. At $5 an hour, that's your pay for the day." Sixty dollars for one day's work seemed like such a large amount compared to the minimum wage I was used to, and it was certainly a far cry from two dollars per job I earned on the Horseshoe.

I went on to work for Mr. Hammond the remainder of that summer and the next. He remained a gruff and tough guy to work for, but he taught me a lot. One day when he dropped me off at home I overheard him tell Dad how good a worker I was. He commented that "he doesn't talk much but he sure does work hard." Overhearing that compliment really made me feel good. In his own way, he mentored me on the virtues of hard work. Years later, in a wheelchair, he attended my major general promotion ceremony in the Pentagon. He swelled with pride when he told me he was partly responsible for my military success. In hindsight, I suppose he was right.

Several years later, my sister Kate and I attended Mr. Hammond's wife's funeral. He was well into his eighties and appeared feeble. He seated on the front pew of the church, and as I walked by to view the open casket, he looked up, smiled, and asked me to sit next to him for a minute. I felt a bit awkward doing so, but out of respect for both him and his departed wife, I honored his request. He leaned over and whispered that he was very proud of me. He apologized for being such a "son of a bitch" to me as a teenager but said he only did so to help prepare me for the future. He teared up when he told me I was like the son he never had. I thanked him for his mentorship and his long and distinguished service to our nation. We never spoke again after that, and a few years later my sister Kate and I attended his funeral in the same church.

In My Element

In the summer of 1968, I attended my first practice for the Central Falcons High School football team. Following a few speeches about safety and hydration, the coach told us to hit the field, and he put us through extensive football drills that consisted of running, exercises, and reviewing blocking and tackling techniques. When practice ended, I noticed a few of the fellas heading my way home, so I joined them. They were new to the neighborhood, so we became fast friends. To ensure we played together, we made a pact to play our first year on the junior varsity, which was expected for most first-year students.

Once the varsity and junior varsity (JV) rosters were finalized, the coach decided to have the JV defense play against the varsity offense as a tune-up for their first game. Since I played both offense and defense, I lined up against the varsity as a defensive end. As the varsity broke the offensive huddle and approached the line of scrimmage, I boldly proclaimed that no one was coming through me on the line! My friends looked at me in disbelief because I was generally very quiet off the field. But playing football is what I loved—I was in my element—and I was determined to show everyone what I could do. The varsity coach was Rocco Romeo, a gruff, no-nonsense coach who was the spitting image of Vince Lombardi, the legendary coach of the Green Bay Packers.

Coach Romeo was not a fan of trash talk and immediately recalled the offense and spoke with them in the huddle. As the offensive line settled down into their three-point stance, it became apparent the coach had directed them to make me eat my words. When the ball was snapped, as if in slow motion, I saw the offensive tackle charge at me, quickly followed by the quarterback handing the ball to the running back with a full head of steam. True to my word, I fought off the block and tackled the running back, with emphasis, in the backfield. As the offense regrouped to call another play, the entire coaching staff gathered to watch what would happen next.

Instead of getting me to quietly bask in my success, showing up the varsity offense spurred me to talk even more. Determined to shut me up and not have his varsity team embarrassed, the coach ran the same play again, and I delivered the same result. Coach Romeo then screamed at the varsity that there was no way a first-year player should beat them. So he ran the same play one more time, and I delivered the same result. At this point, the coach was apoplectic and told the JV team to head inside for showers while he put the varsity players through a grueling and relentless series of practice drills.

The next day I was the talk of the team. My junior varsity teammates were happy about our performance, but the varsity players were chomping at the bit to get another shot at me and redeem themselves. When I arrived at the practice area, the JV coach told me to report to the varsity coach. Nervous and scared that I was in trouble for talking trash the day before, I ran double-time to Coach Romeo to apologize and take my butt chewing. To the contrary, the coach welcomed me to the varsity team and put me in the starting lineup, where I remained throughout my high school years. Making the varsity team as a first-year player was bittersweet. I loved playing with the "big boys" but I was sad to leave my friends on JV.

Five-0

"Where are you boys going?" yelled two policemen cruising by in their official vehicle. My friends and I were walking home from a late football practice and were neither creating a disturbance nor otherwise violating any laws. "Good evening, officer," my friend said. "We're on our way home from football practice. Is there a problem?"

"You don't ask the questions, boy, I ask the questions," exclaimed the officer. "You all stop right there while I pull over." I was raised to respect the police and did so very much but the tone in this officer's voice indicated he was clearly agitated.

I whispered to my friends to just relax and follow their directions. Clearly we had done nothing wrong, so whatever the reason for the stop, we should soon be on our way. The officers exited the vehicle and demanded that we clasp our hands on the back of our heads. They then patted us down, searching for weapons and, I assume, drugs. After finding nothing, the officer stated, "You boys look like football players, but I'm not convinced. There have been several robberies in this neighborhood, and you boys look like you are up to no good." He then hit us with several rapid-fire questions: What school do you go to? What is your coach's name? Why was practice so late? Where do you live? Have you ever been arrested?

As passersby slowed their vehicles and gawked at the group of us, it was humiliating to think our neighbors likely assumed we had committed a crime. As the officers instructed us to turn around and face them, I could not help but notice the firearms they were carrying in their holsters. We were instructed to "not move a muscle" as one of the officers returned to the vehicle and began talking on his car radio. The remaining officer took out his nightstick and simply patted it against the palm of his hand. One of my friends spoke up and said, "Officer, we haven't done anything, can we please leave?"

"Shut up," he said emphatically. "You boys are the ones who have been robbing and stealing around here, and I'm going to enjoy throwing all of you in jail tonight."

The other officer emerged from the vehicle and said, "Just a minute. I'm waiting on a call, and you better hope I don't have to arrest you all tonight. I bet the prisoners in Lorton [a prison in Lorton, Virginia] will love to get their hands on young, strong bucks like you." Suddenly, we could hear the vehicle radio as the offi-cer returned to his car. Without saying a word, the officer hung up the car radio and motioned for his partner to return to the car, and they simply disappeared into the night. My friends and I were both relieved and furious. We had great respect for the police but wondered how those two got to wear the cloth of such a respected organization.

The next day, while dressing for football practice, my friends and I disclosed the events of the previous day to the rest of the team. Since our team was roughly 50 percent white, I was curious about their experiences, so I asked how many of them had been stopped by the police. Much to my surprise, not one hand was raised into the air. I asked the same question to the black players and nearly every hand went up. Coincidentally, I knew several of the white players had been in some serious trouble, both in and out of school, yet none of them had raised the suspicion of local police. I didn't have the chance to dwell on that encounter very long because a week later I was pulled over for no apparent reason while driving the car of a friend. As I had been taught, I was deliberate in my movements and carefully produced the documentation requested by the officer, who subsequently let me go on my way without any indication as to why I was stopped.

Like my friends, my father had given me the "talk." That conversation started out by explaining that most police officers are great people, and we should always, always follow their instructions. There are some cops, however, that are not good, and you have to be careful. So, if you are stopped while driving, keep your hands in plain sight and don't make any sudden moves. No matter how belligerent an officer becomes, don't take the bait. Always remain calm and follow their instructions. Dad was clear that as a young black teenager, I would at some point be pulled over while driving, and he wanted me prepared for that eventuality. What I did not realize at the time was not only would the police stop me as a young adult, but also that being stopped for "driving while black (DWB)" would be a lifelong occurrence. I will forever have great respect for our nation's police force. They have, arguably, one of the toughest jobs in our society and 99 percent do a commendable job. The fear that I and other black males have is the chance of encountering that 1 percent who do not.

Out of My Element

I began my senior year of high school in 1970, just as the United States was beginning its second decade of involvement with the Vietnam War. During the bus ride home from yet another football victory, the topic turned to the war. To a man, my teammates and I were against the Vietnam War, and we swore that we would never serve in the military. Many of my teammates had turned eighteen years of age and, as required by law at the time, had registered for the draft. Still seventeen years old, I asked the coach what he thought about the draft. He responded that although he too did not agree with the Vietnam War, the law is the law and we should all comply.

But he, along with my teammates who had already registered, agreed that if they had to serve in the military, joining the Air Force or the Navy was preferable. The rationale was that if drafted into the Army or Marine Corps, there was a high likelihood of being assigned to the infantry and transferred to Vietnam. The Air Force and Navy, however, were more technical services where one could learn a skill that was easily transferable to the civilian job market. More importantly, even in Vietnam, airmen and sailors were least likely to face any direct combat. Even though Dad had served in the Army, I accepted their argument and swore that if I had to join the military, it would likely be the Air Force because I could not fathom living on the ocean for months at a time.

This was one of many of the daily interactions I had with my coaches and teammates. In fact, discussions with my white teammates became a social learning laboratory. My black teammates and I taught them about the music of James Brown, the Temptations, and Earth, Wind & Fire, while our white counterparts introduced us to musical groups like The Who, Black Sabbath, and the Rolling Stones. In fact, our post–football practice ritual was to sing the song "Hey Jude," a Beatles classic released in 1968. They were also good about explaining terms like "making out," "spaz," and "cool beans," while we reciprocated by interpreting slang terms like, "TCB," "jive turkey," and "brick house."

Football had become my core in high school. It was the only part of my life that made sense. The problem is, once football season ended in my senior year, I had no compass. My report cards were littered with Cs and Ds, and I had SAT scores to match. It's a miracle that I graduated on time; but while walking across the stage during the ceremony, the realization hit me that I didn't know what was next. During the ride home from graduation with my parents, there were no words spoken. Sitting quietly in the back seat, I recalled a comment made by the valedictorian of the class, who said, "As graduating students, we reflect our parents." That epiphany helped me understand that the person I was up to that point in my life was a mirror of the two adults riding in the front seat of our station wagon.

There is only one inscription in my high school yearbook. It says, "Hope to see you playing in the NFL in a few years," signed, "Coach." Despite that lofty premonition, I was adrift after high school. My coaches, who swooned over me during football season, abandoned me after the final game. As a high school graduate, I was no longer of use to them. As a potential college player, my poor grades made me a tough sell for scholarships.

Confusion and Uncertainty

Mom referred to me as a hippie, a 1960s and 1970s term describing young people who subscribed to a counterculture movement that rejected the mores and mainstreams of American life. It was not clear to me at the time that I was part of a movement, but I certainly dressed the part. I had a large Afro hairstyle and dressed in bell-bottom pants and tie-dye shirts. The 1960s and 1970s were a tough and tumultuous time for our country. Antiwar protests, civil rights and women's rights marches, and illegal drugs marked the period. The release of the Pentagon Papers and Watergate eroded the trust and confidence young Americans had in elected leaders.

Jim Crow laws had long been declared unconstitutional, but not every discriminatory action can be regulated, so matters of inequality and bigotry persisted. Socioeconomic and environmental factors and discriminatory housing practices led to de facto segregation that was rampant within inner-city neighborhoods and schools. Debates raged about affirmative action, programs designed to compensate for past discriminatory practices, which some labeled as reverse discrimination, particularly against white males. Demographically, population growth was the lowest in U.S. history and the recognition that the country was turning toward a browner complexion alarmed many in the majority.

This triangle of 1970s environmental factors, parents with no post–high school experience, and poor academic credentials left me confused and uncertain about my future. All my life I had one goal, to play in the NFL, and it appeared that dream would not come to fruition. As one last glimmer of hope, the football coach at Howard University in D.C. was persistent in pursuing my football skills and all but guaranteed I would be a starter during my freshman year. Recognizing my low SAT scores, he offered a tutor to help prepare me for a retest. In hindsight, I should have jumped at this offer. But as the oldest of six siblings and with inexperienced parents, the summer of 1971 simply got away from me, and in early fall I found myself rudderless.

To earn money, I got an entry-level civil service job as a GS-1 with the U.S. Census Bureau in Suitland, Maryland. I also joined a local semipro football league, which is just below the professional level and was nonpaying. It was early September and I was excited about the upcoming NFL season. The Washington Redskins had not made the postseason playoffs in twenty-six seasons, but the hire of new coach George Allen had the city buzzing with anticipation about a potential turnaround.

The Vietnam War dominated the nightly news headlines. September 1971 was the start of Operation Jefferson Glenn, a major ground offensive in Vietnam in which, as television anchor Walter Cronkite reported, the U.S. and South Vietnamese armies had inflicted 2,026 casualties on the Viet Cong and the North Vietnamese army. Lying in bed after the broadcast that night I began to think about my future. I was eighteen years old with no car, no plan, and living in my parents' basement. Playing football was fun, but working in a government job at the bottom salary tier was not the way I had envisioned my life.

On September 19, 1971, I sat in my parents' basement and watched the Washington Redskins defeat the St. Louis Cardinals, 24–17. After the game I started thinking about a conversation with Dad I had had in 1968 as a high school sophomore. Following a high school football game, we were riding home in the car together. During the short trip I asked him why on earth, given the difficult conditions for blacks in the Army during the 1950s, would he fight to re-enlist following his Korean War injury? Clearly, with the loss of his left hand, no one would fault him for leaving the Army. The year 1968 was the height of anti-Vietnam and anti-military sentiment that I had fully embraced, so I suspect he understood that my question had more than a hint of cynicism.

In response, he planted a seed of patriotism that blossomed over time. He acknowledged how tough and unfair Army life had been for his fellow black soldiers and him. But he also explained that his perspective had been shaped by the progress he had witnessed as a black man raised in the South. He told me that as a youngster, he literally feared for his life while in the presence of whites. He also explained that being called a "nigger" was commonplace. But when he joined the Army, he was called a soldier. I had never thought about it before, but the conversation led me to remember and ask the reason he so often wore his uniform while visiting establishments unrelated to his Army duty.

He responded that wearing his uniform garnered him respect, and although, in his opinion, during his twenty years of active duty black soldiers were never treated as equal to whites, he was no longer fearful and, more poignantly, he was hopeful that my siblings and I would not have to endure the hardships he faced. As we turned onto our street and approached our home, he said that he was proud of his service and felt that in his own way he had not only made a personal sacrifice for our country, but he hoped that his example to us proved that the best our country has to offer was still in front of us. He went on to say that although he had never pressed any of his children to serve in the military, he would be very proud if they did so.

This conversation provided a rare glimpse into the person Dad was. He could be gregarious and fun-loving one minute and a stern disciplinarian the next. Underneath that sometimes smooth and oftentimes rough exterior, however, laid a strong American patriot who loved his country. Over time and quite unconsciously, I adopted his love of country and sense of duty. Like my peers in the early 1970s, I reflected the dress and rhetoric of the time. But I never forgot those evenings on the Horseshoe as we watched our parents return home from work. I was the only kid on the block who had a dad in uniform, and that was something everyone on the Horseshoe respected.

4

ENLISTED DURING THE 1970s

Makes me wanna holler and
throw up both my hands.

—MARVIN GAYE [1]

O n October 4, 1971, I made the one-mile walk from the U.S. Census Bureau
to Iverson Mall in Suitland, Maryland. True to the fashion of the time, I
purchased a purple jumpsuit and a matching pair of high-platform shoes. Bags in
tow, I decided to do some window shopping. While doing so, I happened by an
Air Force recruiting office. As I stared at the aircraft pictures through the glass door,
Staff Sergeant Case, who was perfectly groomed and wearing a freshly pressed Air
Force uniform, stepped outside the door, greeted me, and asked if I was a football
player. When I responded yes, he asked me to "come right in and have a seat."

"So you want to play football," Staff Sergeant Case said.

I responded, "Yes, sir, playing in the NFL has been a lifelong dream, but I have
pretty much given up on that."

"How do you feel about the Air Force?" Case asked.

"Well, my dad spent twenty years in the Army, but my friends say the Air
Force provides better training and is a better alternative."

Case agreed. "Your friends are right. The Air Force is a great organization and
has a variety of career fields you can work in, and you can play football."

"Football?" I asked. "How does that work?"

"Well, you can enlist in the Air Force now, complete basic military training, apply for the Air Force Academy, and play collegiate football," Case explained.

"Air Force Academy, what is that?" I asked.

Case responded, "The Air Force Academy is like any other college except it is run by the Air Force. They have the full complement of collegiate sports, and many graduates go on to play at the professional level."

My interest piqued, I asked, "At the professional level? Give me an example."

He responded, "You ever hear of Roger Staubach?" I nodded affirmatively. "He went to the Naval Academy."

"Wow!" I responded. "I had no idea. So, all I have to do is join now and I can play for the Air Force Academy after I graduate from basic training?"

"Yes," Case responded. "Apply for the Air Force Academy and get accepted and you just might fulfill your dream of playing in the NFL."

In hindsight, his discussion of football was crafty, if not outright misleading. His plan was technically feasible, but he did not bother to explain that the Air Force Academy had stringent acceptance criteria that were far beyond my current scholastic grades and SAT scores. Nevertheless, due to a combination of the commitment to serve my country my father had instilled in me coupled with my dream to play football in the NFL, the offer seemed too good to turn down, so, without much forethought, I joined the U.S. Air Force on the spot.

What followed was a fast and unpredictable path to the beginning of my Air Force career in the 1970s. Since my enlistment was totally unplanned and sudden, I decided not to tell my parents right away. Without their knowledge I took a day off from work and traveled on a Greyhound bus to the military induction center in Baltimore for a series of tests and examinations. Following the physical exam, a doctor called me out of the group and told me I had a problem: my weight. My football playing weight was 250 pounds, and the maximum allowable weight for my height at the time was 205 pounds. The doctor explained they had a special weight-loss program in basic military training, but I had to lose 30 pounds to qualify.

I was disappointed with the news but not deterred. When I returned home, I continued to work and play football, but I went on a strict, self-imposed diet and the weight dropped quickly. Exactly three weeks from the date of my physical exam, I lost 30 pounds and was down to 220. I took another day off from work and returned to Baltimore. Since it had only been three weeks, the doctor remembered me and commented that he could tell I had lost weight, but he was skeptical about my claim of the amount of weight loss. So when I stepped onto the scale and the dial settled at 218 pounds, the doctor was stunned but impressed. With my weight no longer an issue, all my paperwork was complete, and I was told to report back in one week to take my oath of enlistment and depart for basic training.

On the bus ride home from the induction center, I realized I could no longer keep this news from my parents. At the dinner table that night I blurted out that I had joined the Air Force and would need a ride to the Greyhound bus station in a few days. Rather than the look of astonishment I anticipated, both parents appeared relieved. As a military man himself, Dad was pleased. He wanted me to earn a college degree, but if that was not in the cards, military service was the next best option. Mom was just happy that I had decided on a course that offered the potential for something positive. As the oldest of six children, I was their first experience of having one of their offspring leave the nest. Perhaps that is why on the night before I departed, Dad hastily arranged our first and only complete family photograph.

An American Airman

On November 10, 1971, I took the oath of office and was officially an airman. My group of new recruits boarded a bus for the short trip to Baltimore-Washington Airport, destined for San Antonio, Texas. During the bus ride I felt a sense of relief. I did not know what the future would bring, but for the first time I felt I had a future. I also thought back on my high school days and the confusion and uncertainty I felt after graduation. I wondered if I had done the right thing. I blamed my parents for our lack of communication and not getting into college, but while gazing out of the bus window I realized I was not being fair. That they had no experience with higher education was not their fault. In time, I reasoned perhaps no one was to blame. I also accepted that the circumstance of my upbringing and socioeconomic condition was the hand I was dealt. With that acceptance, I vowed to play that hand to the best of my ability.

After a short bus ride, we arrived at the airport. I don't know why it hadn't occurred to me before, but I suddenly realized I had never flown on an airplane. In fact, I had never been to an airport. I admit I was anxious when we taxied out to the runway, but when the pilots pushed the throttles forward and I felt the roar and vibrations of the jet engines, I was hooked on the wonder of flight. Climbing through the clouds and leveling off at cruising altitude was dreamlike. The final leg of our flight landed in San Antonio late at night, and my group boarded a bus to Lackland Air Force Base. When the bus arrived, a training instructor (TI) with a very loud voice and wearing a Smokey Bear hat stepped onto the bus, and life as we knew it was about to change forever.

It was 2:00 a.m. when we were hustled into the barracks. There were two separate bays with rows of metal beds and metal floor lockers at the foot of each bed. Rectangular lights lined the ceilings. We were ordered to put our belongings into the lockers, undress, and get into bed, "NOW." Each single bed had a thin mattress that rested on stiff springs. The trainee in the bed next to me was from California. As the TI yelled "lights out," my new friend, in a whispered voice, asked where I was from. Before I could answer, the TI ran in a full sprint to his bed and yelled that since he had so much energy, he could get on the floor and start doing push-ups. On second thought, the TI announced that thanks to our talkative trainee, everyone should "hit the floor for twenty pushups." After we counted out twenty repetitions, a few of the trainees got up from the floor. As we quickly found out, doing anything without our TI's permission would unleash his wrath. So we were ordered to again "hit the floor for an additional twenty pushups."

By the time we finally got to bed, it was around 3:00 a.m. At precisely 4:30 a.m. I was jolted awake from a dead sleep as several TIs came screaming through the barracks instructing us to get up, get dressed, and get outside for morning exercises. It was reminiscent of the old *Gomer Pyle, U.S.M.C.* television series where his drill sergeant would passionately yell, "Move it, move it, move it." As we progressed through the first few days of basic training, I found I actually enjoyed it. Having grown up engrossed in sports, I felt right at home with the discipline and physical fitness routines. Rather than view the TIs as military instructors, they reminded me of coaches that were simply trying to make us better. The precision of drill and learning how to maintain my gear in inspection order came relatively easily.

I graduated from Air Force basic military training in the spring of 1972 but not with my original group of trainees. About midway through the training I entered a special weight-loss program, referred to as the "fat boy" unit, where I lost another 30 pounds. I spent three weeks in this weight-loss unit on an isolated part of the base where we ate in a special weight-loss dining facility and exercised several times each day. After three weeks, I was down from my original weight of 250 to 185 pounds, and I entered another group of trainees that were at the same point in the training period as when I had departed. After basic training, I had a short technical training course at Keesler Air Force Base in Mississippi, followed by a much-anticipated leave to visit back home. In service dress uniform, with a short haircut, and 60 pounds lighter, I suppose it was no surprise when Dad drove our station wagon, filled with my siblings, right past me as I stood staring at them in front of Washington National Airport (now Ronald Reagan Washington National Airport).

North Carolina

Following a short leave period at home, I boarded a Greyhound bus to Fayetteville, North Carolina, for my first duty assignment at Pope Air Force Base. Although I was assigned to an Air Force installation, Fort Bragg Army post dominated the city of Fayetteville. With the backdrop of the Vietnam War, the civil rights movement, and a nationwide drug culture, Fayetteville was a tough town in the 1970s. In fact, soldiers and airmen referred to the city as "Fayette-Nam." The main street leading to the base, Bragg Boulevard, was lined with pawn shops and massage parlors. Large signs offering payday loans and cheap used cars were prevalent. XXX-rated drive-in movies were offered at reduced rates. Vick's Drive-In Restaurant, which featured pork chop sandwiches, fried chicken gizzards, and chitterlings, was a popular eating spot for soldiers and airmen.

My military orders indicated I was assigned to the civil engineering (CE) squadron. Pope AFB is a relatively small installation, in sharp contrast to the large adjacent Army installation of Fort Bragg. Pope AFB was host to several squadrons of C-130 transport aircraft that supported the airborne mission at Fort Bragg. Roughly 150 airmen and civilians were assigned to the civil engineering squadron, which was responsible for maintaining the base infrastructure.

Unlike today, in 1972 there was no sponsorship program to ensure my safe and uneventful arrival at my new duty station, so I was essentially on my own. When I exited the Greyhound bus in Fayetteville, I had no idea what to expect. Apparently, my deer-in-the-headlights look was obvious to a local cab driver, who, observing me dressed in an Air Force uniform, assumed Pope AFB was my destination. Ironically, just as the airplane flight to military basic training was my first flying experience, this automobile ride to the base would represent my first taxicab ride, so I had no idea about fares. As we traveled along the busy streets, I noticed the fare meter clicking up in price. I only had ten dollars to my name, and I began to worry as the fare clicked over that amount. But I said nothing as we arrived at the Pope AFB Personnel Office on a Friday evening after duty hours. Although the total fare was $14.86, I handed the cab driver my last ten dollars. Fortunately, he accepted it and told me not to worry about the rest.

There was an on-duty airman in the Personnel Office who informed me I would need to return on Monday morning during regular hours. In the meantime, he arranged for me to spend the weekend in a temporary room in one of the barracks. With no transportation, I had to drag my duffel bag about three miles to my short-term quarters. At this point, I was really tired, so I went right to bed. The next day, having skipped dinner Friday evening, I made my way to the base dining facility for breakfast. The clerk at the entrance asked for my meal card. I was unfamiliar with a meal card, but I explained my circumstances and requested to eat based on my military ID card.

The dining facility clerk was a stickler for the rules and refused to let me enter. As an eighteen-year old airman with no car, no friends, and no money, I was too afraid to ask for help. As a result, I endured the entire weekend subsisting only on water from the barracks water fountain. When I returned to the base Personnel Office on Monday morning, my first request was for a meal card. My in-processing paperwork took about an hour, and once again I made my way toward the dining facility. With duffel bag in hand, I was in view of the dining facility when a chief master sergeant (the top enlisted rank in the Air Force) spotted me and yelled out, "Hey, airman, come over here."

I turned to see who was yelling at me, and my eyes immediately focused on his arm full of stripes. I had learned about the rank of chief master sergeant in basic training, but I had never actually seen one in person. To say I was intimidated is an understatement. Against my better judgment, I turned away and continued my trek to the dining facility. This time, in an elevated voice, the chief yelled out, "Airman, don't you walk away from me. Come over here now." With little choice, I walked smartly over to the chief, set down my duffel bag, saluted, and said, "Airman Spencer reporting as ordered, sir." I had been taught this reporting procedure in basic training but forgot that it only applied to officers. In my defense, though, at the time a chief master sergeant seemed a lot more important than an officer.

While saluting, I noticed the nametag on his shirt. He was Chief Master Sergeant Brown. Chief Brown said, "Airman, I appreciate the salute but I'm not an officer, I actually work for a living. You must be new to the base."

"Yes, sir," I responded. "I'm just trying to get over to the dining facility for breakfast before I figure out where my new unit is located."

"That's awful," the chief said. "Someone from your unit should have met you. Come with me." Chief Brown walked me to his pickup truck, threw my duffel bag in the back, and drove me to breakfast. I was a nervous wreck sitting at the table with a chief, but he was very kind and helpful.

After breakfast, Chief Brown took me to my new unit and introduced me to the civil engineering chief. That chance encounter with Chief Brown would turn out to be a significant one. He made a point to keep track of me and occasionally stopped by the CE squadron to check on me. This encounter also engendered in me a deep respect for chiefs. As the top enlisted grade, those achieving that rank essentially run the enlisted force, and their service to our country is profound. Fortunately for me, I would run into Chief Brown again, where his mentorship would help set me on a path that, at the time, was unimaginable.

My permanently assigned barracks environment was nothing like I expected. America was engrossed with Vietnam protests, and my barracks mates were clamoring to separate from the Air Force. The stench of marijuana was everywhere. Long hairstyles that significantly exceeded regulations were common. For African Americans, wearing a stocking cap at night significantly suppressed a large Afro into a much reduced and neatly appearing hairstyle. Our white counterparts used a product called Dippity-Do hair gel to disguise their out-of-standard hair length. Uniform appearance was also substandard, which was a far cry from the spit and polish of basic military training.

As I began to meet new friends and settle in to life in the Air Force, I soon found myself in a dilemma. Should I go against my peers and conform to Air Force dress and appearance regulations, or succumb to peer pressure to the contrary? I was only eighteen years old and the peer pressure I felt to be "cool" and noncompliant was intense. While working through the contradictions of becoming an Air Force enlisted member, I discovered that being an airman during the 1970s did not make one immune from the racial prejudices and bigotries of the time.

Racial Tensions

On a late evening in October 1972, my teammates and I were dressed in light athletic clothing to match the mild North Carolina temperatures. As a young enlisted member, I joined my unit's flag football team, and the opposing team was beating us badly. In particular, we could not keep their defensive linemen out of our backfield. By coincidence, the entirety of their defensive line was African American.

As we all stood frustrated and drenched in sweat in our offensive huddle, a white teammate blurted out, "Would someone please block those niggers on the defensive line?"

I was shocked and deeply offended. I was taught that the Air Force did not tolerate that type of behavior and language. Growing up on the Horseshoe I had heard the N-word almost daily, but this was different. This was in a moment of rage. This was in a moment of stress. It was directed at other American airmen who looked like me. It's hard to articulate what that word means to black people in that context. I am aware of its use in black neighborhoods, in popular music, and by comedians, none of which I condone. However, when the N-word is directed at African Americans with the tone and tenor I heard that evening, it creates a wound so deep that even with the passage of time, it is hard to heal.

Fortunately, on that evening I did not have to react or say a word. Despite the palpable look of pain on my face, my fellow teammates came to my defense and severely chastised the offending airman. To make matters worse for my insulting teammate, the defiant statement had been so emphatic and loud that a senior noncommissioned officer, also an African American and referee for the game, heard it as well. The individual was immediately ejected from the game and the incident was reported to his unit leadership the following day.

As I walked back to my barracks room, I couldn't help but think about the incident. I wondered: Despite the frustration during the game, what could have motivated this airman to use that word with such vitriol? I wondered if other airmen felt the same way and express the same language, only in private. I also wondered if my bosses and commanders felt the same way. I reasoned that the airman was just frustrated and upset and simply said something he ordinarily would not say. I reasoned that since others had intervened and condemned the act that this was a random event, an anomaly. I reasoned that this was an unfortunate incident and that I would not have to deal with that sort of bigotry again. Unfortunately, that would not be the case.

After saving my money for a year, in 1973 I purchased my first car. It was a 1968 candy apple red Chevrolet Nova coupe, with monthly payments of $48. Despite my modest monthly pay of $342.30 each month, that car became my financial black hole. I purchased oversized tires and expensive rims, and I supplemented the engine to gain more horsepower. I also installed a stereo system that was probably worth more than the car itself. I handled that car with kid gloves and religiously maintained the scheduled maintenance and washed and waxed it at least once a week.

Late one Saturday evening I was taking a leisurely drive on a back road near Lillington, North Carolina. Suddenly, a pickup truck appeared in my rearview mirror and the driver and passengers were yelling obscenities out the window. My eyes were drawn to the Confederate flag displayed on the front license plate. Like the N-word, despite the affection that some claim for the flag as a symbol of Civil War and southern heritage, the very sight of a Confederate flag strikes fear in the hearts of many people of color, including my own. My initial assumption was I must have been driving too slowly, so I increased my speed. But the faster I accelerated, the faster they drove. I then decided to slow my speed in the hopes they would simply pass and move on.

Slowing down only further agitated them, and by this time they were only inches off my rear bumper. There was no vehicle GPS in the 1970s, so I was really nervous about altering my route, but in an attempt to ditch them, I turned off the main road and headed in a completely unfamiliar direction. Like clockwork, they turned right behind me and continued to yell and honk the horn. Suddenly, my anxiety lifted as I spotted a police car that had pulled a driver over to the side of the road. I slowed my vehicle almost to a stop and pulled off the main road directly behind the police car. At that point, the gentlemen in the pickup truck sped by me while simultaneously giving me the "bird." The last thing I saw was yet another Confederate flag displayed in their rear window.

I remained in my vehicle until the police officer had completed his business, and I motioned for his assistance. He approached my car and asked for my driver's license and car registration. I then explained what had just occurred. His response was that I should not be out driving around "this part of North Carolina" and it was a good thing something worse had not happened. He asked if I had been in trouble with the law, and I replied, "No, sir." He asked me to remain in my vehicle while he ran a check on my license plate. The sun was now completely down, and we were the only two cars on a lonely and dark road.

His eyes were focused on me through his rearview mirror as he spoke into his car radio microphone. At this point, I was really scared. I had done nothing wrong and had done what I thought was the right thing. As if things could not get any worse, I noticed the pickup truck that had harassed me coming back down the road toward us. The driver of the pickup slowed as he approached the officer and he rolled down his window, and they appeared to have a short conversation. Afterward, the officer waved goodbye to the occupants, and they sped past me.

I quickly exited my car and approached the police officer to let him know that that was the truck that harassed me. He immediately turned to me and shouted, "Halt, and don't move another step." I complied with his request, and he began walking toward me while reaching for his handcuffs. I panicked and began pleading with the officer to please not arrest me. I was not being aggressive. At this point I just wanted to get back to the base. Upon hearing the word "base" he asked if I was in the military. I replied that I was indeed in the U.S. Air Force and just wanted to go home. He then asked for my ID card, which I readily showed him. At that point, he told me I was free to go.

Racial tensions among airmen in the 1970s were real. To help alleviate the strain, the Air Force created a Social Actions office that conducted mandatory race relations courses for all airmen. These courses were extremely unpopular and often resulted in heated arguments and debates. The course I attended was no exception. There was a white lieutenant colonel in my session that insisted the course was a waste of time and that blacks should stop complaining. He explained that regardless of what his ancestors may have done, he was not bigoted and resented the mandatory training. A young black captain, who was very respectful of the rank difference, calmly and systematically provided examples of discrimination and bigotry that he personally experienced, and he argued that racial tensions were not just in the past but exist and persist today. Despite the back and forth of that discussion, the course was so unpopular it was eventually discontinued.

My BFF

On a lazy weekend, several of my friends and I decided to take a ride to the local town of Erwin, North Carolina, where the girlfriend of one of our friends resided. When we arrived, there were several other young women in the house. An introvert, I was generally shy around women, but one of them, Ora Mae Cameron, caught my eye. Ora was a tall, slender young woman with a great smile. Unlike the others, she was not brash or loud; rather, she was very nice and appeared to be a bit shy. I approached her and started a conversation that led to a constant stream of dates and phone calls. She lived about thirty miles from the base, so I put hundreds of miles on my Nova going to see her.

Over time, Ora became my best friend. We were nineteen years old and neither of us had a clue what we wanted out of life. Despite our young age, late one night while taking a ride in the Nova, we decided to get married, and so we did on April 29, 1973. She was a bit apprehensive about marriage and was considering joining the Army, but she agreed, and we secured a license and got married at a local courthouse without the knowledge of either of our parents. We rented a run-down, one-bedroom apartment just outside the base for $85 per month. She had to leave her job to join me near the base, so money was extremely tight. There was no air conditioning and our only heat source was turning the oven on high heat and opening the door. Most annoying, the house was infested with mice.

Growing up with roaches and rodents on the Horseshoe, I learned to detest mice. But our new apartment living room was a virtual skating rink for mice at night. I literally lay in the bed and watched them scurry around like they owned the place. When I complained to the landlord, his response was to put down mouse-traps. I was determined not to share my apartment with mice, so I embarked on a mission to rid our house of these unsanitary and unsavory creatures. Following a full house inspection, it was clear that the rodents entered the house at night through several holes in the floor under the sink. I patched them as best I could, but no matter how hard I tried, those noxious rodents found a way to make their nightly visits into our apartment.

Despite those conditions, life was simple and we were happy. It was just the two of us, and we shared everything. I often think about how brave Ora was to run off with someone with such an uncertain future. She had grown up in a small town, and I knew she wanted something different. She wanted to see the world and experience new things. Her ticket out was to join the Army, and she had envisioned her life as a soldier stationed overseas. But I had abruptly and unceremoniously disrupted her plans. She was very close to her family but now had to spend most days alone when I left for work. Over the years, her support and love never wavered. She is by far the most loving and compassionate person I have ever known. I have wondered how her life might have turned out if I had not walked through her friend's door that day. For me, it is very fortunate that I did.

After just a few months in our apartment, Ora informed me she was pregnant, and our first son, Larry II, whom we call by his middle name, O'Neil, was born on August 19, 1973. Neither of us was prepared to be parents, but I suppose most young couples feel the same. Having a son was a surreal experience, and I could hardly wait each day to come home to be with him. When O'Neil was about two months old, we received a bombshell: Ora was pregnant again. Then we received another bombshell when I was notified of a remote deployment to Ching Chuan Kang (CCK) Air Base in Taiwan, which meant I would be away from my new family for an entire year.

The timing of this news could not have been worse. It's hard to put into words how difficult it was to leave my new family for an entire year, especially with Ora being pregnant. We had been married less than a year and had an infant son and another on the way. Two nineteen-year-olds, we were not prepared for a separation. Studies have shown that young military members often marry at a young age to replicate the family structure they left. I suspect that was the case with me, as the news of a yearlong deployment was the toughest life challenge I had faced. I appealed to my first sergeant to at least delay my departure until after my second child was born, but the request was denied.

Eight-Thousand-Mile Journey

Out of options, I packed what few belongings we had, moved Ora and O'Neil to her parents' home in Dunn, North Carolina, and made the eight-thousand-mile journey to Taiwan. We arrived in the main city of Taipei at night and were taken directly to a hotel. The next morning, I pulled back the curtains to the hotel window and gazed outside. This was indeed a new world for me. Small vehicles with horns honking dodged around dozens of bicycles on the busy street. Senior citizens performed rhythmic exercises on the city sidewalks as morning workers hurried past. We boarded a bus for the three-hour journey to my new assignment for the next year. The main highway was a single lane with two half-size lanes on either side and no speed limit. We gasped as the large bus barreled down the highway, only to veer off to the side for an approaching vehicle at the very last second, and then right back into the center lane.

I was assigned to the base Post Office. As an E-2, I lived in a dormitory room with no air conditioning, no television, and no radio. My first purchase in the base exchange store was a can of bug spray. After escaping an apartment infested with mice, I was now assigned to a barracks with some of the largest cockroaches I had ever seen. To combat the large pests, I developed a system of applying bug spray along the bottom of the room door at night, and inevitably there would be at least one dead roach, lying feet up, on the floor in the morning. My room had a bunk bed, and even though I didn't have a roommate, I slept on the top bunk, somehow believing the roaches would stay on the lower part of the room.

One night, I had a dream that one of those large creatures crawled across my face. The horrifying thought of those tiny feet on my face woke me from a dead sleep. I lay there in bed cringing at the thought and feeling thankful that it was just a dream—or was it? The more I thought about it, the more it bothered me. Just to be sure, I jumped out of the bed and turned on the light. Thankfully, I didn't see anything in the bed, that is, until I lifted my pillow, and there he was. This huge cockroach, with big feet, was looking at me as if to say, "Would you please cut the light out, so I can get some sleep?" I never slept quite as soundly after that.

My first visit to the local town of Taichung was a memorable one. The homes were small by American standards and packed tightly together. Large water buffaloes pulled carts packed with vegetables and fruits along the back streets. The downtown area was lined with nightclubs and side-street eateries. Whole cooked ducks and chickens hung up by their necks were prevalent in the food display areas. Vendors of all sorts competed for airmen's attention to stop by their establishments to have a suit made or to paint a portrait. The nightlife was like a scene from Harlem during the 1950s. Nightclubs were lit up with neon signs, and scantily dressed women enticed airmen to enter.

Adjusting to being "remote" and away from my family was difficult. To help take my mind off the separation, I joined the base basketball team. Playing on the base team was a healthy distraction and provided the opportunity for my teammates and I to travel the entire island playing various American and local basketball teams. I also developed a group of great friends that helped ease the stress of family separation. It was, however, 1974, so it was difficult to escape issues of race, even halfway around the world.

The Harlem Globetrotters?

Quite by chance, the entire base basketball team was African American. During an overnight stay at an away game in the capital city of Taipei, several of my teammates and I went out for dinner at a local restaurant. Most of the patrons in the restaurant were local Taiwanese. Since several of my teammates were at least six feet tall, I was not surprised that we got more than a few stares. But they seemed innocent enough, and no one on our team gave it a second thought. As we proceeded to our table, we noticed a group of what we assumed to be U.S. military members. As we walked by their table, one of them yelled out, "These must be the Harlem Globetrotters. It's bad enough I have to watch them on television, but I'll be damned if I have to eat with them."

The center on our team, who happened to be about six feet, eight inches tall and not a person I would tangle with, approached the table and asked if there was a problem. Our tall center went on to say we were not the Globetrotters but rather in the U.S. Air Force. The loudmouth at the table responded that they were in the U.S. Air Force as well and that a "group of black guys should not travel in packs late at night because people will assume they are up to no good." After restraining our center, we found a table across the room and enjoyed dinner. As one can imagine, though, the dinner conversation was dominated by the incident and we were all disgusted at what had taken place. We were particularly disturbed that these were not random people off the street; these were airmen.

An Angel in Uniform

Working and playing basketball helped dull the sense of loneliness and homesickness, but the thought of not seeing my family for a year was almost overwhelming. I truly believe that God intercedes in times of need, and I was desperately in need. While eating lunch in the base dining facility one day, my intercessor walked through the door. A1C Frankie "Mad Dog" Maddox was stationed in Okinawa but was on temporary duty in Taiwan. We had been friends back at Pope AFB and I was elated to see him. Maddox got the nickname "Mad Dog" because he was fond of a cheap but available wine called Mad Dog 20/20. When Maddox spotted me, he came over to my table, and we quickly renewed our friendship.

Maddox was indeed a godsend. We spent most of our free time together, and his companionship is just what I needed to take my mind off the loneliness. Maddox remained in Taiwan for three months and it was a sad day when he departed, but that ninety-day respite provided the additional distraction I needed to complete my tour. Twenty-eight years later, I walked into the base exchange store at Langley AFB, Virginia. I was the comptroller for the Air Combat Command and had recently been selected for promotion to brigadier general. As I perused through the store aisles, I could hardly believe my eyes. It was Mad Dog Maddox, now retired and working in the store. "Mad Dog, is that you?" I asked with a bit of hesitation.

"Larry, how the heck are you? I haven't seen you since Taiwan."

Mad Dog and I reminisced for about an hour when he asked me to wait just a minute. He went into the back room and returned with an envelope. Inside the envelope were pictures of him, our friends, and me when we were stationed together at Pope AFB. I was amused to see a picture of myself wearing my old high school letter jacket and sporting a much out-of-regulation hairstyle. He then showed me a newspaper article. It was the announcement of my promotion to brigadier general. I asked why he had not contacted me. He replied that he just didn't think it would be right for a retired master sergeant to contact a general officer. The next day I went out of town on business for two weeks, but as soon as I returned, I tried to find Mad Dog in the store to rekindle our friendship. The store manager told me Maddox no longer worked in the exchange, and I never saw or heard from him again.

My yearlong deployment completion date was October 15, 1974, but on July 17 our second son, Derrick, was born. I immediately requested leave to go meet my new son, but my request was summarily rejected. Air Force policy at the time was if the birth of a child was normal and uneventful, it was not deemed an emergency and thus leave was not authorized. I offered to take regular, rather than emergency leave, but my boss said that since I only had ninety days until my return home, he could not let me go. I was distraught and upset over this decision, but I had no choice. So I was forced to rely on pictures sent through the mail until my tour was complete.

Knob Noster

Following a five-hour flight from Los Angeles, after nearly a year away from my family, I flew into Washington, D.C., for a short visit with my parents and to pick up my car. The five-hour drive to Dunn, North Carolina, was filled with great anticipation, but when I walked through the door of my mother-in-law's house, it was as though I had stepped into a fantasy. Ora was overjoyed to see me, as I was to see her. To the right of her, in the middle of the floor, were a one-year-old and a three-month-old staring at me like I was a complete stranger. From their perspective, I *was* a stranger, and my deep voice startled them. But after a few weeks of playing and getting to know me, it was as though I had never left.

With the excitement of my return, I forgot to mention where we were going next. Ora asked, "Are we moving back to Pope AFB? If so, we should drive down and find a house." I responded, "Not exactly. We're moving to Knob Noster, Missouri, which is where Whiteman AFB is located." Since she had never been out of the state of North Carolina, her response was, "Where is Missouri?" Not to disparage the small town of Knob Noster, but for a guy from D.C. this was literally in the middle of nowhere. There was one blinking light that controlled the center of the town, and there was no shopping, no McDonald's, no nothing. Whiteman Air Force Base, however, was responsible for leading a wing of intercontinental ballistic missiles, which sounded exciting.

Two things that nonmilitary families may not appreciate are the difficulties associated with frequent moves and the strain of assimilation back into the family unit following a long deployment. When we arrived at Whiteman, as an E-3, airman first class, I could barely afford the one-bedroom trailer we rented in a local trailer park. Living in such tight quarters with little disposable income and a thousand miles away from family and friends was tough. Also, having served overseas for a year, reintegrating into my family proved challenging. During my time away, Ora paid the bills, disciplined the boys, and generally ran the home. Trying to step back into those duties or, God forbid, criticize how they are done, can and does put a large strain on a marriage. But over time we worked through those challenges.

A Pivotal Exchange

An unexpected challenge was that my Afro hairstyle was becoming difficult to disguise. While stationed in Taiwan, I managed to go an entire year without a haircut. In Knob Noster, Ora braided my hair during weekends, but compressing the girth during the week by wearing a stocking cap at night was increasingly problematic. On a Monday morning, I was the first to arrive at the Safety Office where I was assigned. I looked up from my desk as a chief master sergeant walked by and only casually looked at me through the door. A few seconds later, that chief was at my desk and emphatically asked, "When was the last time you had a haircut?" After stumbling through my response, the chief directed that I come with him.

Much to my surprise, the chief did not appear angry or upset. He calmly took me to his truck, drove me to the base barber shop, paid the barber, and said, "Give him a regulation haircut; he looks terrible." As I watched my hair fall on the barber shop floor, I couldn't help but notice the smile on the chief's face. Following the haircut, the chief drove to the base park and shut off his truck engine. "Your name is Spencer, right?" he stated.

"Yes, sir," I replied.

The chief continued, "I've seen you around and you appear to be a very good worker, but you had to know your hair was way out of standard."

I replied, "Yes, chief, it's the style and all my friends are doing the same thing."

The chief then made a statement that really caught my attention: "So why is it that you want to follow rather than lead? It's hard to believe but I was once young, so I understand the peer pressure to follow the crowd, even when you know it's wrong. But you are an airman now. We have standards that must be upheld. If you want to leave the Air Force and grow long hair, then do it. However, if you want to remain in my Air Force, you need to follow the rules. Is that clear?"

"Yes, sir, chief," I replied. "You are right, and I won't let it happen again."

"Okay," the chief said. "I won't mention this to your boss. But tell me something, you seem like a bright guy, are you enrolled in college courses?"

"No, but I have thought about it."

The chief responded, "Okay, let's stop thinking about it and visit the base Education Office and get you enrolled." This was a pivotal moment in my life. I enrolled in a local college on the spot and began my journey to earn a bachelor's degree. Working during the day and attending school at night was tough, but the more I studied and read, the better grades I achieved. I began to realize I was just as smart as anyone else and in many cases maybe even smarter. For the first time in my life, I realized that my lack of academic performance in the past was the result of not understanding how to study. Now that I was scoring As on my exams, my confidence level soared. My newly developed study habits also helped with my work performance, as I earned a promotion to E-4, sergeant.

During this period, I rediscovered my passion for cost savings and efficiency, which resulted in a boost for my family and career. As a sergeant, I was eligible to move out of my trailer home into base housing. Doing so meant a larger home for less money, plus utilities were included. The shorter work commute meant I saved money on gas and we were closer to the base commissary and base exchange store. We also took advantage of the local thrift shop for secondhand clothes and the auto hobby shop, where I serviced my own vehicle. Like father, like son, there was an area on base for family gardens, so I planted and harvested my own vegetables.

This passion for cost efficiency also led to a career change. As I progressed with my college work, I found my assigned career area of administration was less challenging. So I started exploring options to cross-train into another field. One of my course instructors was a young first lieutenant who suggested I try his field of financial management and offered a tour of his unit. When I told him about my love of saving money, he offered me a project to complete. The assignment involved a review of the grounds maintenance and office refuse collection contracts, both of which had become increasingly expensive. The lieutenant had an intuition that both contracts were inefficient, and he asked me to conduct a deep dive to determine the facts.

My review found that the grounds maintenance contract included open fields of weeds rather than actual grass. Similarly, the office trash removal contract specified emptying trash cans in offices that no longer existed. My recommendations were simple: remove the grounds that did not have grass from the contract, delete the nonexistent offices from trash removal, and direct members to empty their own office trash where it made sense to do so. The projected savings were modest, but this opportunity renewed my passion for cost efficiency. As a result, I applied and was accepted to retrain into financial management, which resulted in yet another assignment change to Charleston AFB, South Carolina.

To Re-enlist or Not?

Charleston AFB is considered a plum assignment because of its proximity to beaches and the beautiful surrounding historic cities loaded with southern charm. The primary mission of the base was operating a wing of C-141 transport aircraft. I performed well in the financial management field and was promoted to E-5, staff sergeant. I also continued with my college studies, played on the base basketball team, and played first base on my unit's intramural softball team. My life was beginning to take shape, and I was starting to believe I had a good future. Charleston AFB, however, is in the South, and no matter how well I performed as an Air Force noncommissioned officer, once again I had to deal with racial biases.

Late one summer evening during a tight intramural softball game, the batter hit a sharp ground ball toward our shortstop. Our shortstop was talented and quickly scooped up the ground ball, checked the runner at second base, and fired a bullet directly toward me at first base. The force of his throw was such that the ball made a distinct "pop" as it hit my first baseman's glove. Immediately, the first base umpire emphatically called the runner out. The bewildered batter was frustrated and got into the umpire's face to protest the call. He then surprisingly said to the umpire, "Just ask the first basemen, he will tell you that I was safe."

Since the umpire had made the call, I was focused on getting ready for the next batter, but in an uncharacteristic move, the umpire turned to me looking for reinforcement of the call. Not quite sure how to handle the situation, I simply spoke the truth, that the batter was indeed out, and I added "by a mile." The batter then turned his ire toward me and stated that "niggers don't know anything about baseball, so you should play basketball instead." I am not proud to admit that in the heat of that moment, I lost it. I immediately charged after him, and the only thing that saved me from getting into real trouble was that he could run faster than I could.

My teammates and those watching from the stands found the episode quite amusing. I suppose the sight of me chasing a person half my size around the outfield was a sight to behold. To add to the humor, the batter jumped the outfield fence and continued to run and never looked back. I returned to my first base position, a little winded from the chase, and the game continued. As I leaned forward into my first baseman's stance waiting on the next pitch, the thoughts of the incidents at Pope AFB and CCK AB came flooding back. This time my reasoning was not so idealistic. It was clear that this person harbored racist beliefs that he kept hidden until a stressful event forced his true feelings to the surface. Don't get me wrong; I am not naive. I know there are racists in our country that come in all shapes, sizes, colors, and ethnicities. But this individual was also an American airman, a fact I could not so easily reconcile.

In November 1977 I had a decision to make: re-enlist in the Air Force for another four years or separate and seek civilian employment. That decision got really complicated when my civilian boss, a graduate of Clemson University, called me into his office. He said that the Clemson football coaches had seen my high school tapes and wanted me to visit the school for a tryout. I walked out of his office on cloud nine. I had long ago set aside my dream of playing football in the NFL, but suddenly that dream came back to life.

I had a week to decide about re-enlisting, and I tossed and turned at night wrestling over my choices. To help decide, I employed an old technique I had used in one of my college courses. I took a sheet of paper, drew a line down the middle from top to bottom, and labeled the two columns Clemson and Air Force. I then listed the pros and cons of each choice. Clearly I was emotionally invested in pursuing my football dream, but with a young family to think about, it was hard for me to envision attending school full time, playing football, and supporting my family. So at the end of the week, I visited the local personnel office and re-enlisted.

This was in effect the end of my dream of playing professional football, but I was at peace with the decision. At the same time, though, I established another dream: earning my college degree. I committed myself to completing my degree prior to the end of my new enlistment period and to be prepared to separate from the Air Force with the credentials to land a good civilian job. During my formal re-enlistment, I discovered I could request reassignment to a base location of my choice. I chose to return to Pope AFB, North Carolina, so Ora would be near her parents and because Pope AFB offered an on-base degree program from Southern Illinois University (SIU) in industrial engineering technology. Based on my passion for efficiency and cost savings birthed from my youth on the Horseshoe, this degree seemed like the perfect fit.

During the summer of 1978 we made the short journey from Charleston to Fayetteville, North Carolina, and purchased a small home in the local community of Spring Lake, North Carolina. O'Neil turned five and started school. I began working my Air Force job in financial management during the day while attending college courses at night and on the weekends. This was an intense period and one of great family sacrifice, but I was single-minded and determined to complete my degree. On weekends, SIU professors traveled from Carbondale, Illinois, to teach the core curriculum. These courses consumed full days on Saturday and Sunday. To complete the electives associated with my degree program, I had to complete noncore courses at local colleges during the week and at night.

Keeping up this pace was exhausting and oftentimes discouraging, but in September 1979, I graduated at a small ceremony on base, which my parents attended. Ironically, the same Chief Brown, whom I encountered during my initial assignment to Pope, had also returned and was now the senior enlisted leader for the entire base. When he heard about my graduation, he decided to attend the ceremony. Following graduation, the chief asked me to stop by for a visit. I was a bit nervous standing outside his office; but when I entered, his positive and supportive comments put me at ease. He asked if I was interested in applying for Officer Training

School (OTS) and becoming an officer. Before I could respond, he listed several advantages to taking this path, which included higher pay and greater opportunities to lead.

I don't know why, but I didn't think I had a snowball's chance of being selected for OTS. I had a long family history of military service, but none in my family had ever achieved officer rank. The application process was a bit cumbersome, but I was pleasantly surprised by the support and encouragement I received from family and friends. In a month or so I received the news, and it was good. I was elated when my boss informed me of my selection to OTS. Based on my first choice, I would remain in the financial management career field. Obtaining my college degree was a long-held dream that came true for me. Becoming the first military officer in my family's history was a dream come true for my entire family lineage.

5

AN OFFICER AND A GENTLEMAN

My goal was to make first lieutenant.
I never spent a lot of time worrying
about what came after that.

—GEN. HUGH SHELTON (RET.)[1]

My flight landed at the San Antonio, Texas, airport on November 10, 1979, and I didn't know quite what to expect. Ironically, it was eight years to the day after I had arrived at the same airport for basic military training (BMT) and now I would attend Officer Training School (OTS). In November 1971, I arrived for enlisted BMT with a group of trainees, and we were herded and yelled at the minute we stepped off the airplane. My arrival for OTS came with no such fanfare. No one met me at the airport, and I had no instructions. Like the other passengers on my flight, I walked to the baggage claim area, retrieved my luggage, and caught a cab to my home for the next ninety days at Medina Annex at Lackland AFB, Texas.

I walked onto the OTS campus and was met by an upperclassman, which meant he had completed the first half of the training. I was assigned to class 80-06, with a graduation date of February 14, 1980. As an active-duty staff sergeant, the first order of business was the uneremonious removal of my stripes. All incoming enlisted airmen were ushered into a small room where another upperclassman literally cut off our stripes with a razor blade. We were quickly divided into groups of "flights" consisting of about twenty-five trainees and assigned two to a room.

Following an anxious wait in our barracks, we met our training instructor for the duration of our training.

Second Lt. Carol Mercer was sharp, focused, and dedicated to the mission of OTS. Mercer was a model officer in every respect and was all business. Small in stature, she was large in talent and leadership. My roommate was Officer Trainee (OT) Doug Norman. Our initial conversation was nothing like I experienced in BMT. Chatter among fellow BMT trainees was mostly about sports, girlfriends, and making it through BMT. During our first night as roommates, OT Norman talked about bees. I initially found that subject a bit odd until I discovered that Norman had recently completed a study of bees and was excited to tell me all about the results.

Like BMT, I thrived in OTS: the drill, sports, academic requirements, physical fitness, and leadership . . . I loved it all. The differences between OTS and BMT were stark. The yelling and barking out commands in BMT were replaced with firm but respectful communications. Rather than "Airman this" or "Airman that," we were addressed as Mister or Miss. Rather than having a noncommissioned officer watching our every move and telling us exactly what to do and when to do it, OTS used a different approach. As officer trainees, more self-accountability was expected. We had plenty of rules and guidelines to follow, but we were expected to figure them out on our own.

Following an anxious first night of sleep, I was awakened by the sunshine that peeked through the blinds covering the single window in our room. I glanced at the small alarm clock sitting on the single nightstand, and it read 6:00 a.m. This was our first full day at OTS, and I wanted to be ready for whatever was in store. At precisely 6:30 a.m., Lieutenant Mercer greeted us at the door. With a loud bang, she knocked once and entered the room. Norman and I snapped to attention. She handed us a manual and said she would return in one hour for our first room inspection. Norman attempted to ask a question for clarification, and Lieutenant Mercer firmly and with great clarity repeated, "I will return in one hour to inspect your room—is that clear enough for you, Mister Norman?"

We, along with the remainder of our flight in the dormitory, quickly cracked open the manuals and studied the fine art of folding underwear and making beds with "hospital corners," which involves a forty-five-degree angle fold on both sides of the mattress at the foot of the bed. This was old hat for me so I was not at all intimidated. There was no broom, so we improvised by attaching a strip of masking tape along the side of a yardstick for sweeping. In exactly one hour, Lieutenant Mercer returned with white gloves and began the inspection. She didn't say a word, but the look on her face told us we had not aced our first inspection. After inspecting each room, she directed the entire flight to "fall out" on the sidewalk to march to breakfast. Thus began our ninety-day journey to become Air Force officers.

Lieutenant Mercer was all spit and polish and a stickler about uniform appearance. Every day before classes began, she inspected each of us up close and personal. Our ritual was to stand at attention as she entered the classroom and face away from our desks. She then inspected every inch of our uniforms and yelled out for us to give ourselves a demerit when she found a discrepancy. As a fierce competitor, I was determined to not allow Lieutenant Mercer to find one discrepancy with my dress and appearance. This frustrated Lieutenant Mercer to no end, so it became a daily competition between the two of us. On day five of our training, I cracked an internal smile as Lieutenant Mercer looked me up and down and moved to the next classmate. She then abruptly returned to my position, squatted down, and glared at my shoes for what seemed like several minutes. She then yelled out for me to give myself a demerit for a "speck of dust on my shoes."

That evening I spent an hour polishing every inch of my shoes. While doing so, I thought of an idea to ensure my room remained in inspection order throughout the duration of our training. After placing my newly spit-shined shoes under the bed, I carefully folded my garments, ironed them to perfection, and properly arranged them in the locker. I then made my bed for the last time during my three-month stay. From that point forward, I used only the underwear and towels stowed in my laundry bag. I also scrounged an extra blanket to use at night as I slept on top of the perfectly made bed.

As OTS ended, we conducted peer evaluations, which were anonymous and designed to help each officer trainee see how others perceived them as trainees and future officers. Much to my surprise, I received the top ranking in my flight. Two of my classmates wrote, "Officer Trainee Spencer is a future general officer." I had racked up numerous class awards, including highest academic average and a number of athletic awards. The icing on the cake was an announcement that I was the sole distinguished graduate in our flight, which meant I graduated in the top 10 percent of our class. OTS was clearly a turning point in my professional career and my life. I had finally shaken off the negative baggage from the Horseshoe and was brimming with confidence.

Immediately following graduation, I hitched a ride to the San Antonio airport and arrived at Dulles International Airport just outside D.C. around 8:00 p.m. Dulles is about thirty-five miles from my parents' residence, so I asked Dad to meet me at the air-port. When I stepped outside, Dad was standing next to his car waiting. Since I departed from OTS quickly, I was still in uniform as a brand-new second lieutenant. As I approached the car, Dad walked around from the driver's side of the car to greet me. He said, "Congratulations, lieutenant," and then saluted. His father had enlisted and served during World War I. He had enlisted, served in the Korean War, and retired after twenty-two years. His siblings enlisted in the U.S. Army, U.S. Marine Corps, and the U.S. Navy, but no one in our family had ever become an officer. Although he struggled to verbally express it, he was deeply proud of me as the first.

Georgia on My Mind

Following graduation in February 1980, my family and I borrowed Dad's station wagon and made the drive to my first duty station as an officer, Robins AFB, Georgia, where I was assigned to the Air Force Reserve Headquarters. As a family, it was our first experience in the Deep South. To my great fortune, my new boss was a complete gem who prepared and launched me on a successful career. From day one, Lt. Col. Frank Tuck took me under his wing. Tuck was bright, had an impeccable work ethic, and spent an inordinate amount of time mentoring me. Among other things, Tuck taught me to be "eager and enthusiastic," a phrase and concept that I now pass on to those I mentor. Tuck set the performance bar high and pushed me to exceed it. He taught me the technical aspects of the job and how to be an officer and leader.

I had not given much thought to being assigned in the South until Tuck took me around the base to meet folks he felt I should know. One of those was a senior, crotchety colonel who led the base financial management organization. Try as I could, it was hard for me to ignore that this gentleman spit the remnants of chewed tobacco in a can on his desk and spoke with an exaggerated southern drawl. As we took our seats in his office, I was shocked as he began to hurl racial epithets like it was acceptable. I don't think he intended to offend me, although I can't imagine how he could have thought otherwise.

His bottom-line advice to me was to make sure I "minded my manners" and not act "uppity" and I would get along just fine. During this "advice" I glanced over at Tuck, who was equally appalled and embarrassed. On the car ride back to the office Tuck apologized profusely for the colonel's behavior and said it was fortunate that the colonel would be retiring soon. As a brand-new second lieutenant, I grimaced at my own naive belief that I had left these racial attitudes behind in the 1970s.

Another challenge involved my new secretary. On the first day in my new office my secretary informed me that she had no experience working with a black man and that I made her nervous. I eventually won her over, but she confided that her family was not happy that she actually worked for me. There was also a senior civilian on the staff that seemed to avoid me at all costs. Eventually, I confronted him to determine if I had somehow offended him. Much to my surprise, he unashamedly told me that he "loathed blacks" and wanted nothing to do with a black officer. I later discovered that he was an active member of a white supremacist group that apparently trained with high-performance weapons somewhere in the deep woods of Georgia.

One warm spring Saturday morning our family visited the base park to toss around a football. I threw a long pass to my son Derrick and it sailed over his head into a children's play area. As Derrick ran over to retrieve the football I noticed he paused for a quick conversation with a young kid about his age. I also noticed an adult in uniform interrupt their conversation. When Derrick ran back with the ball, he asked me what the word "nigger" meant. I was taken aback but tried not to show any concern. This was a word we never used, and he was confused. He said the adult that had just interrupted his conversation with his classmate said he didn't want his kids playing with "niggers."

Assimilation

I am often asked about the contrasts between enlisted service and becoming an officer. While there are both similarities and differences, the most immediate challenge of becoming a second lieutenant was assimilation. The enlisted ranks are wholly diverse. So when attending organization events and activities, those in attendance were racially and ethnically diverse, with both men and women represented. The officer ranks, however, particularly at the senior grades, are far less diverse. As African Americans, Ora and I had to navigate the waters of being the only blacks in the room throughout my career.

For example, Ora and I were excited when we received our first invitation to attend a unit social event in the Officer's Club. The timing was shortly after my arrival to Robins AFB, and we looked forward to meeting other families in the unit. We entered the designated room in the club and it was immediately apparent we were the only black family in the group. As we made our way through the crowd, it was as though they were speaking a foreign language. It was springtime and my counterparts seemed to be obsessed with the game of golf. We constantly heard terms like tee boxes and greens that left us scratching our heads. I was asked a dozen times about my handicap and had no idea how to respond.

As we struggled to keep up, the band started playing country music. I have nothing against country music, but I had not been raised to appreciate that genre. Soon our counterparts began singing along with the band. Feeling awkwardly out of place, we tried our best to lip sync songs we had never heard. As the evening progressed, the alcohol flowed, and conversations wandered into politics. Whereas Ora and I are politically moderate and don't strongly affiliate with any political party, it was simply assumed that as officers we exclusively supported right-wing positions. For most of the evening, we heard "left wing" this and "Democrats" that. We were not particularly offended by those comments, but their presumption about our political views was annoying.

The challenge of assimilation is not unique to the military, but it was a bit frustrating that there appeared to be no understanding of or appreciation for the assimilation process. Our preferences in music or recreation or political leanings were assumed. We felt as though we had to abandon our culture and adopt another, to be people we were not. That first social engagement was a painful reminder of how my parents employed their "white voice" when in the presence of whites in an attempt to sound proper and speak like them. It was as if their normal speech would be interpreted as crude, slang, or unsophisticated.

Making My Mark

As a freshly minted second lieutenant I was anxious to make my mark. Shortly after I arrived, the Air Force Reserve commander held a conference for his subordinate commanders. During the conference, the field leaders bitterly complained about the number of reports required by the headquarters. They lamented that it was hard to get their work done while constantly responding to headquarters' taskings. After hearing about this, I raised my hand and offered to take this on. Since

I was the lowest-ranking person in the room, there were more than a few looks of skepticism. But when I explained my vision for "Operation Paper Wait," our major general commander gave me permission to proceed.

The first task was to list all reports the field believed had been levied on them by the headquarters. Concurrently, I went to each headquarters office to get a list of the reports they required from the field. Finally, I reviewed the reports that were submitted to determine their value. Surprisingly, the two lists did not match. There were reports submitted by the field when there was no requirement and the headquarters required reports that the field did not respond to. Also, many of the reports required by the headquarters had little if any value. In several cases I visited a headquarters office to review a report, only to find no one had read the document and it was filed away in a cabinet.

When we presented the results of our analysis to the commander, he was frustrated with the findings but ecstatic over the work. We recommended eliminating eighty-three reports, which would save 18,000 hours of work each year, and the commander fully endorsed our suggestions. This was followed by a study to centralize computer resources, which saved $150,000; development of a comprehensive ninety-page pocket-sized information digest on the Air Force Reserve while eliminating five previously unused publications; and an investment equipment study that saved $50,000. Because of these and many other cost-savings initiatives, I was awarded the Meritorious Service Medal that read in part, "Lieutenant Spencer's efforts resulted in over twenty cost reduction initiatives and management enhancement studies that produced documented savings in excess of one million dollars."

During another routine staff meeting, not only was I the junior person in the room, but also the lone African American, so there was little diversity of thought during their discussion. The commander and his staff were deliberating over an issue involving the status for Air Reserve technicians who were concurrently civil service employees. During the hand wringing, I gingerly spoke up with an idea to help solve the problem. The initial reaction was a "thud," but several minutes later the commander paused the discussion and asked me to restate what I had suggested.

Having heard me a second time the staff also took note. After a few seconds of silence, the commander asked, "Why didn't we think of that?" As it turned out, that one act resulted in far-reaching benefits for me because despite my junior rank, the commander began asking for my opinion more frequently and expanded my level of responsibility. To be sure, my suggestion was not rocket science, but it clearly was nontraditional. This experience highlighted the importance and value of diversity, not just variety of race and gender but of background and experience that allows different ideas and approaches to complex issues to be viewed through varying life experiences and lenses. With Tuck as my boss and mentor, my young career was off to a great start, so it was bittersweet when he informed me of his promotion to colonel and a reassignment to Andrews AFB, Maryland.

Based on the opportunities Tuck afforded me, in 1981 I was selected as the Air Force Cost and Management Analysis Officer of the Year. This was a significant award that was rarely awarded to a lieutenant. The downside (or at least at the time I considered it a downside) was that the award got me noticed by the top brass in the Pentagon, who shortly thereafter selected me for reassignment to the historic building. I departed Robins AFB with mixed emotions. Professionally, I could not have asked for a better boss and mentor. Assigning a first lieutenant to the Pentagon, however, was an anomaly and a challenge for which I was ill-prepared.

The Pentagon

The Pentagon is headquarters of the United States Department of Defense (DoD). It is a 6.5-million-square-foot office building with approximately 23,000 military and civilian employees and about 3,000 nondefense support personnel. In addition to five sides, it has five floors above ground, two basement levels, and five ring corridors per floor with a total of 17.5 miles of corridors. A little-known fact is that as construction of the Pentagon was done during racial segregation, dining facilities for blacks were in the basement and there were double toilet facilities separated by gender and race. As a result, today the Pentagon has twice the number of toilet facilities needed for a building of its size.

One statistic the Pentagon could not claim was an abundance of lieutenants. In fact, assigning a lieutenant to the top headquarters in the DoD was rare. The Cost and Management Analysis Directorate had established a new field support branch, and they wanted an officer with field experience. Despite my junior grade I was their choice. Walking into the Pentagon for the first time, I felt like a mouse dodging around the feet of bull elephants. The hallways were filled with top brass and "action officers" scurrying around coordinating packages for their bosses. If the work pace at Robins AFB was 60 mph, the Pentagon was traveling at 200+ mph! It was rare to see a military officer below the grade of lieutenant colonel, so I had to run twice as fast to keep up.

My first challenge was financial. The D.C.-Maryland-Virginia (DMV) area is expensive, and my lieutenant's salary offered few options. The only home I could afford was about twenty-five miles south of the Pentagon in Dale City, Virginia. Anyone who has braved D.C.-area rush-hour traffic understands that a twenty-five-mile commute can easily take an hour or more on normal days. Add an accident or bad weather and there was little hope of arriving in under two hours. Today, carpool lanes offer much-needed rush-hour relief for those willing to commute as a group. Also, a practice known as "slugging," whereby commuters simply show up at any one of several carpool parking lots and hitch a ride, has significantly improved the commute. But things were different in 1982. There was no Metrorail; there were no slug opportunities, and carpool lanes extended only halfway to Dale City.

A distressing story I heard about the Pentagon that gave me pause was the infamous heart attack cart. Purportedly this emergency cart boasted a minimum transit time to reach a heart attack victim anywhere in the Pentagon. The lore of the story was that the high stress level in the Pentagon made those assigned particularly susceptible to heart attacks. I assumed the story was urban legend until I got to witness it in action during my very first week. To minimize the effects of the elevated stress levels, I established a personal routine of exercising each day during the lunch hour at the Pentagon Officers Athletic Club (POAC).

One day, following a vigorous basketball game, I had undressed and was walking toward the shower when I heard a commotion. As I moved closer, I saw a middle-aged man lying on the floor, and he appeared to be unconscious. Sure enough, the heart attack cart quickly arrived. As the medical team started CPR, I caught a glimpse of the man's face, and I recognized him. We had served together at Pope AFB when I was an enlisted airman and he was a major. As I later discovered, he had been promoted to colonel. The medical team continued to administer CPR as they lifted him onto the cart and sped away. I was saddened to learn the next day that he had passed away.

When I arrived at the Pentagon, my two sons were in elementary school, and my daughter was born shortly after my arrival. I spent what little weekend time I had being active with my son's little league activities, but in hindsight it was not enough. Since I worked so far away from home, I could not attend school activities or parent-teacher meetings. The mental and physical demands at work were difficult and took a toll. There were days when I was physically at home but mentally in the Pentagon. To cope, exercise was my refuge. Seven days a week, whenever possible, I either ran or lifted weights. If it is possible to be addicted to exercise, I was hooked.

Professionally, my time at the Pentagon was rewarding. I worked with some great military and civilian people, many of whom I would work with again in my career. I was assigned projects normally reserved for those of much higher rank and experience. As a result, I established a strong record of performance and reputation as an officer with a bright future. Socially, we very much enjoyed the Washington, D.C., area. From the great monuments and historic sites to the recreation areas and parks to professional and college-level sports, the region of the nation's capital offered a plethora of family activities that, as time permitted, we took full advantage of.

As my four-year assignment ended, I was ready to leave. I was burned out from the late nights and frequent weekend work. Since OTS graduation, I had worked as a cost analyst, but it was well known that the budget field offered the best growth opportunity. So my boss arranged for me to change career paths and be reassigned to Military Airlift Command (MAC) at Scott AFB, Illinois. After the drive from D.C. to the area of Illinois east of St. Louis, I dropped my family off at a rented house outside Scott AFB and traveled alone to Sheppard AFB, Texas, for budget analyst training. I enjoyed budget school and graduated as the single "honor gradu-ate" in the class. A welcomed respite during the course was a visit from my son Derrick. We shared my room and spent some quality time just hanging out during my off time. That time alone with Derrick reinforced the thought that although I had done well in the Pentagon, I wondered if the sacrifice of family time was worth it. I vowed that I would never return to the Pentagon—a vow I would not keep.

Stress-less

On a summer night in 1988 at 9:00 p.m., I was in the cockpit of a C-141 trans-port airplane. I had been assigned a major project of planning a trip to the Pacific theater for the vice commander of Military Airlift Command (MAC), and we were on our last leg of the return. We were fifteen minutes out from landing at Scott AFB, Illinois. Since we had flown nonstop from Hawaii, we were low on fuel. I was buckled into a "jump seat," just behind the pilot and copilot. While on descent over St. Louis, the copilot reminded the pilot in an anxious voice of the low fuel level. I listened intently on the aircraft headphones as the air traffic controller from Scott AFB vectored the large cargo plane onto its final approach.

Without warning, we went into a sharp left bank as the pilot was hopping mad. The vector took us too far off course and much too close to the runway. The controller apologized as we broke through the low cloud deck and recommended we go around for a second approach. The copilot quickly responded that our fuel level was critically low and that we needed to land now. The pilot pushed the aircraft toward the center runway lights as the copilot said, "I see the rabbit," a reference to the flashing runway lights that are quickly sequenced in a forward motion like that of a running rabbit. We were dangerously close to the runway as the pilot fought the balance between a nose-down decent and flaring the nose to get the fuselage wheels down on the runway. We touched down in the dark of night, and the pilot immediately engaged the thrust reverser switch while firmly applying the brakes. My eyes were as wide as silver dollars as we came to an abrupt stop at the very end of the runway.

My assignment to Scott AFB introduced a personal challenge I did not expect. Quite unknowingly, the intensity of work in the Pentagon had become my new normal. Working multiple projects with short deadlines gave me a rush, and the more reasonable pace at HQs MAC felt like withdrawal. My body and my mind were in a hurry to get someplace but there was no place to go. As a new budget officer, I was given a modest account to manage, but the slow pace was so frustrating I made up work just to keep busy. I prepared spreadsheets, analyzed every dollar, and was generally a pest, constantly asking for more work.

This behavior drove my civilian boss and coworkers bonkers. To help fill the void, I became a volunteer personal financial counselor, enrolled in a master's degree program, and spent hours in the gym. There is an old rap song by Kool Moe Dee titled "I Go to Work." The song lyrics talk about the intensity of his work ethic. I epitomized those lyrics. Over time, my zeal for more activity forced my boss to counsel me about slowing down. He complained that I overanalyzed my programs and worked late when there was no need to. At one point, I even volunteered to write articles for the base newspaper. I was a mess.

Today I chuckle when I read my performance reports during that time, which have descriptive words and phrases like "Outruns any work schedule" and "Thrives in a fast-paced environment." The heartbeat of the budget directorate was Budget Operations, also known as the Engine Room. I requested a move to the Engine Room, and my boss agreed only if I would continue with my current portfolio. That meant I would do the work of two, and I happily agreed. As it turned out, the Engine Room was just what I needed. Lt. Col. Jack Tarascio was my new boss, and he was great. Tarascio was smart, supportive, and fun to be around. Jack eventually retired as a colonel but clearly should have been a general officer. Even as an inexperienced budget officer, after my first year in the Engine Room I was selected as the Military Airlift Command's Budget Officer of the Year.

BTZ

The promotion path from second lieutenant to first lieutenant and then to captain is predictable. If the performance levels are good, nearly everyone gets promoted on the same cadence. Promotions to major, lieutenant colonel, and colonel, however, are more nuanced. For those grades, a small percentage is set aside for below-the-zone (BTZ) promotions. BTZ promotions were designed to identify those performing at such a high level as to warrant accelerated promotion ahead of their peers. While uncommon, BTZ promotions are available for each of those grades. In fact, nearly everyone promoted to general officer achieves at least one BTZ promotion during his or her career.

While neither a BTZ promotion nor becoming a future general officer were thoughts or goals I entertained, Lieutenant Colonel Tarascio pointed out that my performance track record from Robins AFB, the Pentagon, and now at HQs MAC clearly stood out and would make me competitive for an early promotion to major. He explained that for promotion to major only, one could be promoted as soon as three years ahead of his or her peers, although that was indeed rare. As I settled in to my new role in the Engine Room, I enjoyed the excitement of developing and executing the budget for a large Air Force command, but I gave absolutely no thought to an early promotion.

In mid-July 1987 I was home watching the Major League Baseball All-Star Game on television when our director of budget, Col. Ed Gunderson, called and asked if I could come into work. The Pentagon had just directed a major budget reduction in response to Gramm-Rudman-Hollings legislation and the HQs MAC commander wanted a briefing first thing the next morning. Colonel Gunderson and I developed a justification package to curtail the reductions that the commander promptly approved. While walking back from the commanders' office, Colonel Gunderson asked me to follow him to his office. When I entered, he thanked me for my work on the budget package and informed me that I had been selected for promotion to major, three years below the zone!

I was thrilled with the news but a bit naive about its significance for my future. For starters, the BTZ promotion meant I was concurrently selected to attend an in-residence professional military training school. Also, whether it is deserved or not, officers selected for early promotions are managed more intensely than those promoted on the regular schedule. When high-profile vacancies occur, oftentimes BTZ officers are identified to fill those vacancies. So, much to my surprise, when a vacancy occurred in the HQs MAC four-star commander's suite, despite the previous practice of selecting up-and-coming pilots for the vacancy, I was selected to fill the billet.

My new boss was a lieutenant colonel and a C-130 pilot. On my first day in the office he let me know his first choice for the job had been a fellow pilot. He further questioned my ability to be successful in the job and referred to me as a "finance puke." If those comments were not insulting enough, he suggested that most "support" (nonpilots) officers rarely get promoted above the grade of lieutenant colonel, so I would be lucky to get one more promotion after this one.

Since I was the junior major selected for promotion in the Air Force, it was tradition to organize the majors' promotion celebration for the entire base. As Ora and I greeted those entering the Officer's Club for the festivities, a major C-141 transport pilot I recognized from the gym congratulated me, but with a caveat. He said he was happy about my promotion, but he didn't understand why the Air Force would "waste" an accelerated promotion on a nonpilot.

My early selection for promotion to major came with a selection to attend the Marine Corps Command and Staff College in Quantico, Virginia. I had always admired the Marine Corps and thought it would be great to spend a year with them. As I reflected on my tour at Scott, the beginning was a bit rough because I had to adjust to a slower pace. But even though I had to take on two jobs, that pace was more to my liking. And I got promoted early and had the opportunity to be the first nonpilot assigned to an elite job in the command secretariat. With that experience behind me, it was time to experience the Few, the Proud, the Marines.

Semper Fidelis

"Leadership is like a pole full of monkeys. If you are on the top of the pole looking down, all you see are smiling faces. If you are on the bottom looking up, all you see are rear ends." That was one of the many pearls of wisdom I received from my primary instructor at Marine Corps Command and Staff College, Lt. Col. Mel Martello. My selection to attend the school was an honor and a unique privilege. I spent an entire year immersed with Marine Corps officers, studying the intricacies of the Marine Air Ground Task Force (MAGTF). While at the Marine Corps Command and Staff College, everyone, regardless of military branch of service, had to meet Marine Corps standards of fitness. Whereas the Marine Corps physical fitness test was a bit more strenuous than the Air Force test, all twelve of the Air Force officers assigned scored in the top tier during the test. As a bonus, several in our class organized an over-thirty basketball team to compete in the base league, where we won the base championship.

Early in our training, we were given a take-home exam that involved both friendly and hostile forces. Our task was to organize a battle plan to defeat the enemy. Because this was a new experience, I wanted to do well and impress my classmates. I stayed up all night, carefully laying out my war strategy on a large poster board. I was proud of my work, and with no sleep I arrived in the classroom early and put my poster on an easel, covered it over, and went out for coffee. When I returned, my classmates had arrived, and the instructor asked me to be the first briefer. When I confidently stood up and removed the cover from my poster board, much to my surprise, some of my classmates had altered my plan.

First, someone wrote on my plan that the first thing an Air Force unit would look for after taking the beach was a nice hotel, so they drew a picture of a Ritz Carlton on my poster. They said the next thing an Air Force officer would do was build an Officer's Club, so they drew a picture of a club and called it "The Air Force Palm Beach Inn." Finally, they said securing a beachhead was interesting but after finding a hotel and club, Air Force officers would call in their Red Horse construction units to build a golf course, so they drew an eighteen-hole golf course, complete with greens, tee boxes, and club house. You could hear the laughter throughout the building, but I was not at all amused. Despite the lighthearted prank, I scored well on the test.

Overall, my experience at the Marine Corps Command and Staff College was great. I met some very dedicated, smart officers and made some lifelong friends. I came away from that experience with an enduring respect for our U.S. Marine Corps and an awareness that Americans can sleep well at night knowing their U.S. Marine Corps is on the ready. The experience also reinforced my respect and confidence in the U.S. Air Force. In all strategy sessions, the capabilities the Air Force brings to the joint fight were front and center. I can't imagine any conflict that the Air Force would not be among the first to arrive and the last to leave. God only knew that my next assignment would put that recognition to the test for the entire world to see.

Desert Shield/Desert Storm

I was excited about my follow-on assignment to the 4th Comptroller Squadron at Seymour Johnson AFB, North Carolina—my first command. Command is a unique opportunity that is only afforded to a fortunate few. I hastily departed Quantico Marine Base because the commander I replaced was due to retire. Attending a professional school for nearly a year did not afford me the opportunity to take any time off, so my plan was to take command, allow my predecessor to depart, and take a few days off. But that was not to be. Just as I arrived at my new command, the war drums of Operation Desert Shield/Desert Storm began to beat. Since the United States had not deployed to war since Vietnam, there were few that thought it would happen. Once it became apparent our country was committed to war, those of us assigned to Seymour Johnson AFB were pressed into action.

Seymour Johnson AFB was perfectly positioned as a point of embarkation for forces crossing the continental United States en route to a myriad of Middle East locations. Airplanes, cargo, and troops traversed the base day and night. As the wing's comptroller, I was responsible for funding our portion of the war effort and ensuring the financial viability and fiscal integrity of our deployed locations. Between preparing members of my own squadron to deploy to working on the out-processing line helping others to shipping checks and cash overseas, on some days I literally worked twenty-four hours straight. As the senior financial manager on the base, I was the person families turned to for assistance with their personal finances. In response, we delivered several briefings in the base theater explaining financial benefits and offering advice on how to manage financial obligations while spouses were deployed.

Shortly after the deployments started, a senior officer above me responsible for logistics and supply was tasked to deploy. That thrust me into the position of being both wing comptroller and acting deputy commander for resources. Suddenly I found myself managing the wing's financial affairs during the day and marshaling cargo and supplies at night. I marveled on the flight line at night as one loaded C-141 cargo aircraft got airborne just ahead of empty airplanes landing. Throughout the initial deployment to the actual start of hostilities, I was heartened by the dedication and hard work of the entire wing, but I was especially proud of those in the 4th Comptroller Squadron.

Money is not something that immediately comes to mind when entering a war, but I know from firsthand experience that you don't go to war without it. From purchasing aviation fuel to food to individual troop pay, the demands for financial support during war are daunting. One morning at 2:00 a.m., I was driving through the base when I noticed a light on in one of my finance buildings. Assuming someone had left the lights on after a long day, I entered the building to turn them off. Much to my surprise, an Air Force civilian, Ms. Gerrie Walker, a GS-5 in charge of civilian payroll, was working to ensure that everyone was paid on time. She never complained and, unbeknownst to me at the time, never asked for overtime pay. She had a job to do, and she did it. That was typical of the people assigned to my squadron, and I was never prouder of them.

Desert Shield/Storm took a toll on all of us, but in the end it was well worth it. There is nothing like total and swift victory, and that is exactly what United States and coalition forces achieved. As U.S. forces began returning home, the well-deserved break we anticipated was not to be. Processing thousands of troops back stateside was nearly as hectic as deploying them forward. Thousands of travel vouchers had to be processed and paid, and special pays such as hazardous duty pay had to be discontinued. Local fuel stocks needed filling and supply bins needed replenishment. As dozens of commercial airplanes landed at Seymour Johnson, we set up pay booths to quickly complete the financial affairs for our returning troops.

Once the main effort of the war subsided, we got back to normal operations of budget and finance. On a Friday afternoon, I arrived home a bit early. Ora and the kids were out shopping, so I had the home to myself. I walked into the kitchen, grabbed something to eat out of the refrigerator, and reached across the countertop to open the microwave door. In doing so, I quickly turned to my right and saw a police officer, inside my home, with his gun pointed directly at me. He ordered me to drop what I had and raise my hands above my head. I complied with his request and carefully and cautiously asked why his gun was pointed at me.

He replied that an alarm had been triggered at my residence, and when he saw me enter my front door he assumed there was a robbery in progress. I was a bit taken aback since I was dressed in my Air Force uniform. I explained that we did not have an alarm system, so his explanation did not make sense. He then called on his police radio and asked for a clarification on the address. The radio response indicated the alarm was from another home on the same street. The officer then lowered his gun, walked out the front door, and departed. There was no apology or acknowledgment of the mistake. In hindsight, I understand that mistakes happen, but not even offering a simple "I'm sorry" was inexcusable in my view.

Saving Money

With the intensity of the war behind us, I set my sights on cost savings and efficiencies. We initiated a cost-savings tiger team to examine unneeded and wasteful spending. Our team examined everything from contract services to what some believed to be an unnecessary flight line dining facility. The results of this team were spectacular. All totaled, the group saved $450,000 in one year that was applied directly back into the wing's high-priority requirements. The results were so impressive that the Air Combat Command (ACC) comptroller paid us a visit to personally review our results.

During that visit, the ACC comptroller mentioned that the Air Force was considering a test to decentralize funding for aviation fuel. The premise was that Air Force wings would be more judicious with aviation fuel consumption if they had to manage a budget, compared to the current centralized distribution method, which led to little accountability. To sweeten the deal, any wing that volunteered could keep any savings generated locally. Once I heard that, I convinced our commander to let our wing test the concept. We were given an allocation of fuel funding based on historical usage and were challenged to manage to that consumption level or below.

Since there was little computer automation at the time, fuel tracking was largely manual, to the point where in many cases we literally tracked small paper receipts around the globe. As the test got into full gear, I flew on several missions with our KC-10 aircraft crews to see firsthand how they could adjust speeds and altitudes to save fuel. We made this test a wing-wide effort, and the results were spectacular. During the first six months, we were saving so much money that the headquarters adjusted its policy of letting us keep the savings locally, stating that it was too much money for one base to spend. In all, we saved $1.4 million, about half of which we kept locally for base improvements.

With this and other successes, word spread about the great support efforts of the 4th Comptroller Squadron. As a result, when the Air Force level awards were announced, the 4th Comptroller Squadron was named "Best in the Air Force," and I was named "Best Comptroller in the Air Force." The following year, our wing aced a major inspection and our squadron led the way as the highest rated in the wing: "Outstanding, Best Comptroller Squadron Seen to Date." That rating in large part led to the 4th Comptroller Squadron being named "Best in the Air Force" a second year in a row, an accomplishment that had never been achieved before and has not been achieved since. I was honored and humbled by the recognition, but the credit clearly goes to the hard-working men and women, both military and civilians, of the squadron.

In addition to the great folks in my unit, I was indeed fortunate to work for a wing commander that was a great role model and mentor. Col. Hal Hornburg and his wife Cynthia set an impeccable example of leadership, professionalism, and grace for Ora and me. At that point in my career, no financial manager had ever become a wing commander, but their example put a burning desire inside me to someday, somehow, follow in their footsteps. I worked hard during that assignment, and Colonel Hornburg rewarded me with high ratings. Even so, I was both surprised and humbled when Colonel Hornburg informed me of yet another below-the-zone promotion to lieutenant colonel and selection to attend the Industrial College of the Armed Forces (ICAF) in Washington, D.C.

Industrial College of the Armed Forces (ICAF)

We were excited to return to the Washington, D.C., area the summer of 1993. ICAF is one of several senior DoD schools designed to provide graduate-level education to promising senior officers. ICAF is a ten-month military education program at Fort McNair in Washington, D.C., that focuses on our nation's industrial base and features several trips. My group had the opportunity to travel to Wall Street in New York and to both England and Germany. Much to my surprise, ICAF also included a competitive sports program that I took full advantage of.

In addition to intramural sports competition, ICAF offered varsity teams in softball, basketball, golf, bowling, and track and field. The primary competition was between the two senior-level schools at Fort McNair: ICAF and the National War College (NWC). NWC is like ICAF except it is more operational than industry-focused. In addition, all the senior military schools—Army War College, Navy War College, Air Force War College, and so on—participated in a three-day, intense sports competition called Jim Thorpe Weekend, held in Carlisle, Pennsylvania, over the Memorial Day weekend. Both the academics and athletics were

My grandfather, Charlie Spencer (P.A.), in uniform
before departing for World War I. *Personal photo*

Looking dapper in the basement of our home on the Horseshoe. My siblings and I looked forward to new toys at Christmastime. *Personal photo*

My dad, Alfonzo Spencer, in uniform prior to departing for the Korean War. This is our only photo of Dad showing his left hand, which was amputated during the war. *Personal photo*

My dad, Sgt. Alfonzo Spencer, shown at
Forest Glenn Annex laboratory, Washington, D.C.,
demonstrating his prosthetic limb. *Personal photo*

Ora and I met for the first time in Dunn, NC, 1972.
Personal photo

Ready to head to downtown Taichung City while stationed in Taiwan in 1974. Taichung City is noted for its night markets and lively club scene. *Personal photo*

Left to right: My son Larry, 2nd Lt. Larry Spencer,
and my son Derrick attending my brother
Leland's wedding in Baltimore, MD. *Personal photo*

Promotion ceremony to lieutenant colonel while assigned to Seymour
Johnson AFB, NC. *Left to right:* then-Col. Hal Hornburg,
Lt. Col. Larry Spencer, wife Ora Spencer. *Personal photo*

Attending a Christmas Party while assigned to the White House.
Left to right: Lt. Col. Larry Spencer, First Lady Hillary Clinton,
President Bill Clinton, wife Ora Spencer. *White House photograph*

Ora and I greet mentor and friend Gen. Lloyd "Fig" Newton upon his aircraft arrival at Tinker AFB, OK. General Newton was the first African American pilot on the Air Force Thunderbird Demonstration Team. *U.S. Air Force photo*

Building a snowman with daughter Shannon. We received a big snowfall during our first week of my assignment to Hill AFB, UT, as Wing Commander. *Personal photo*

My one-star pin-on ceremony at Bolling AFB, D.C.
On the left is mentor and friend Maj. Gen. Robert
"Bob" Smolen. *U.S. Air Force photo*

Viral photo of my two sons, Larry (*left*) and
Derrick (*right*), pinning on my 4th star during a
ceremony in the Pentagon. *U.S. Air Force photo*

Ora and I attend an event on Capitol Hill
with mentor and friend Gen. Colin Powell.
U.S. Air Force photo

With my mother
Selma following a
speech at her former
high school in 2013.
Courtesy of The
Farmville Herald

With one of my favorite football players, Hall of Fame quarterback Doug Williams, during a Washington Football Team practice. *U.S. Air Force photo*

With the late Senator John McCain during a Capitol Hill ceremony to recognize 2nd Lt. John R. Pedevillano as he received the Presidential Unit Citation for his service during World War II. *U.S. Air Force photo*

My most memorable Capitol Hill meeting with the late Congressman John Lewis. He was indeed an American hero and patriot. *U.S. Air Force photo*

Friend and colleague Sheryl Sandberg, Chief Operating Officer for Facebook. I had the pleasure of meeting Sheryl during a Pentagon visit and was very impressed with her intellect and compassion. *U.S. Air Force photo*

It was an honor to be part of this photograph with three other African Americans born and raised in Washington, D.C., who achieved 4-Star rank. The photo was taken in my Pentagon office, with a picture of a Tuskegee Airman in the background. *Left to right:* Adm. Cecil Haney, USN; Adm. Paul Reason, USN; Gen. Lester Lyles, USAF; and me. *U.S. Air Force photo*

Ora and I stand with President Barack Obama in the White House. I had the honor of meeting with President and Mrs. Obama several times, both during and following active duty. *White House photo*

It was an honor to walk out to the mound and hand the baseball to pitcher Stephen Strasburg to start a Washington National's playoff game. *U.S. Air Force photo*

I was humbled and honored at the unveiling of the Air Force General Larry O. Spencer Innovation Award with then–Secretary of the Air Force Deborah James. *U.S. Air Force photo*

Following an on-stage interview with Jeff Bezos for the
Air Force Association annual Technology Symposium.
I found Mr. Bezos to be very engaging and
appreciative of military service. *Personal photo*

challenging, but I thoroughly enjoyed the course, graduating as a distinguished graduate (top 10 percent) and earning a master of science degree in industrial resource management.

The White House

I departed ICAF the summer of 1994 to my follow-on assignment, which was a dream opportunity: the White House. Working in the White House was not just a once-in-a-career opportunity; it was a once-in-a-lifetime experience. My official duty title was Assistant Chief of Staff, White House Military Office (WHMO). My job was to assist the chief of staff in managing the operational activities of more than 1,800 joint military personnel and more than $120 million in direct support to the president. WHMO units included the Air Force One aircraft and staff, the Marine Corps presidential helicopters, Camp David, White House Communications Agency, White House Medical Unit, and the White House Staff Dining Mess, to name a few.

Job tasks ranged from working with the White House counsel on military-related legal issues to briefing congressional subcommittees on the budget to traveling with the president on Air Force One. The quality of those assigned to the White House staff is exceptional. Every employee is handpicked and must pass a thorough security clearance, so the staff is the proverbial all-star team. Work in the White House is busy and oftentimes stressful but at the same time thrilling. Viewing the president's daily schedule gave me insight into the rigors and stresses of a U.S. president that few get to witness. I had great respect for the office of the president prior to my assignment to WHMO, but the opportunity to be a backbencher during high-level discussions heightened my respect for that office.

An unanticipated bonus was serving under the WHMO director, Al Maldon. Maldon was an impressive leader who, in addition to being a retired Army colonel, was well-versed in legislative matters and was someone less experienced White House staff members leaned on for advice. Perhaps the best testimony of Maldon's leadership was the admiration he garnered from those lowest on the rank structure. One of my daily duties was to track the schedule of the White House motor pool drivers, most of whom were young Army enlisted members. Throughout my interactions with them, they consistently commented that despite Maldon's elevated status, he always made time to speak with and support them.

During my tenure, I had an interesting case of mistaken identity that involved two Catholic nuns. Although our normal dress was civilian attire, in WHMO, Wednesday was uniform day. So on a beautiful spring Wednesday afternoon, I decided to take a walk on the Pennsylvania Avenue side of the White House, where I encountered two very nice Catholic nuns. They both took one look at me and exclaimed, "Oh my, it's General Colin Powell." I smiled and told them that although I was a great admirer of General Powell, he had served as an Army four-star general and I was an Air Force lieutenant colonel. They both seemed a bit perplexed but surmised that for security reasons, I could not reveal my identity. So they quietly asked if I would pose for a picture, and I accommodated them. I've often wondered if to this day they have their picture with "General Powell" hanging over their fireplace mantel.

A unique and fun springtime opportunity was dressing in a bunny suit and participating in the annual White House Easter egg roll on the South Lawn. I invited my ten-year-old daughter Shannon to accompany me. Prior to the official event, I took Shannon on a private tour of the White House. The military assigned to the White House and those assigned to the Secret Service enjoy a special and close relationship. So when I asked the on-duty Secret Service agent if Shannon and I could peek inside the Oval Office, he was very accommodating. As we peered inside the majestic office, I mentioned to Shannon that if she remained focused on her academic achievements, she, too, could one day sit behind the Resolute desk of the President of the United States.

Without any hesitation, my ten-year-old daughter responded that I should know better than to suggest that a black woman could be President of the United States. I was visibly shaken by her comment. We had raised Shannon to believe that if she was willing to do the work, she could achieve any life goal she desired. That brief yet impactful encounter, though, showed me the damage that is inflicted on young people of color and young women who are bombarded with negative stereotypes that get deeply rooted into their psyches.

After a year or so into my White House tour, Al Maldon was transferred to another White House assignment. His replacement was a former Marine Corps colonel, Alan Sullivan, who in turn hired a new deputy for the office, Col. Jim Hawkins of the Air Force. Hawkins was a wonderful leader who became a mentor and friend, so it was more than fitting that he notified me of yet another below-the-zone promotion to colonel and selection on the Mission Support Group Command list. A Mission Support Group commander is akin to a city mayor. The leadership duties include base security, personnel management, facilities and grounds upkeep and maintenance, information technology, and base recreation and morale activities, which include clubs, gymnasiums, and child care facilities.

In May 1996 I received a phone call from a mentor and friend who had previously served as vice commander to Colonel Hornburg during my time at Seymour Johnson AFB. Brig. Gen. Silas "Si-Bob" Johnson was commander of the 552nd Air Control Wing at Tinker AFB, Oklahoma, where he commanded a wing of E-3 Sentry aircraft. The aircraft are distinguishable by the large dome on the top of the aircraft fuselage. The wing had undergone tough times and morale was low. Johnson was an exceptional leader and was brought in to right the ship.

"Hey, man, what are you up to?" Johnson said.

"I'm fine, sir," I responded.

Johnson continued, "Congratulations on making the group command list. Do you want to know where you are going?"

"Sir, absolutely if you know."

"You're coming to Oklahoma. The way this base is organized, I don't run the base. However, I asked the center commander to pick you because there is a lot of work to be done, and you're the man to get it done." I was extremely grateful to General Johnson for the opportunity and told him he would not regret the confidence he showed in me. This would be my biggest leadership opportunity to date, and I was chomping at the bit to get started. I immediately called Ora and told her we were moving to Oklahoma. Her response was, "Oklahoma! You must be kidding."

Before I departed the White House, I experienced a special treat. During my tenure I had often seen President and Mrs. Clinton either traversing the White House, departing the south lawn by helicopter, or at special events like the annual Christmas party. By tradition, however, when military members departed presidential service, President Clinton made a concerted effort to personally greet them and take a picture. Additionally, those military members assigned inside the White House were afforded the benefit of an Oval Office meeting with family members.

I could feel the butterflies in my stomach as my family and I entered the Oval Office. Entering the majestic office space and viewing the resolute desk gave me a feeling of walking into history. President Clinton is a tall man with a warm and inviting smile. Some in the media had created an impression that the president did not like the military, but that was clearly not my experience. In fact, my experience was that the president very much respected and admired the military. I crisply walked toward the president, shook his hand, and introduced my family. We all chatted for a few minutes, snapped some pictures, and departed. This short but memorable encounter was a fitting end to this once-in-a-lifetime assignment.

6

FULL BIRD

Never tell people how to do things.
Tell them what to do and they will
surprise you with their ingenuity.

—GEN. GEORGE S. PATTON[1]

y promotion to the rank of colonel, often referred to as full-bird colonel, was a significant milestone in my career. Some had said colonels run the Air Force, and I was excited to become a leader at that level. I also knew this would be a big deal for Dad, so when I notified him, he could hardly wait to tell his former Army enlisted friends. After I broke the news, like a bolt out of the sky Dad handed me a book titled *Firefight at Yechon: Courage and Racism in the Korean War*, by Lt. Col. Charles M. Bussey (Ret.).[2] He simply asked me to read it and said nothing more. Lying in bed that night, I opened the book and began to read. The book chronicled the Korean War experience of then First Lieutenant Bussey, and it made the case that many black soldiers and officers did not receive the proper recognition for their service during the war.

I found the book to be very interesting, and Bussey's portrayal of actual combat events was graphic and stark. As I viewed the pictures in the center of the book, I was surprised to notice the photography credit for many of the pictures was "A. Spencer/77th Engineer Combat Company." As I read further, two pages of the book stopped me in my tracks. Those pages, along with a follow-on conversation with Dad, finally revealed the answer to my lifelong mystery of how he lost his left hand. During the Korean War, Dad was assigned to the 77th Engineer Combat Company, where his primary duty was operating and maintaining a D-7 bulldozer. His company commander was Lt. Charles Bussey; and as an additional duty, Dad was the company photographer.

On November 20, 1950, Sergeant Spencer was ordered to transport his bulldozer to the town of Kunu-ri, North Korea, a distance of about a hundred miles. Such a trip normally involved loading the bulldozer onto the company "lowboy" (flatbed truck) for transport. But, unfortunately, the flatbed truck was inoperable, so the company commander ordered Dad and a fellow soldier, Sergeant Munroe, to drive the bulldozer, as slow as it was, the entire one hundred miles. As the two soldiers began their long, slow journey, alone and in extremely cold conditions, severe fatigue and sleep deprivation set in, and for a brief moment Dad fell asleep, lost his balance, and fell off the moving bulldozer onto its tracks.

A bit dazed and before Sergeant Munroe could stop the dozer, his instinct was to roll off the vehicle tracks onto the ground. In the process, the dozer tracks ran over Dad's left forearm. The bulldozer track severely crushed his hand, and he was left with no immediate medical care and only his fellow soldier for comfort. Facing an excruciatingly painful and severe injury and harshly cold temperatures, Dad fell into a coma, his mangled hand became gangrenous. He remained unconscious until he was finally rescued days later and transferred to Japan for the surgery that amputated his left hand.

I asked Dad about this experience, and what he remembered most was a dream. While in a coma, he needed an iron lung (now called a ventilator or respirator). During that period, he vividly remembers dreaming of cutting down a large tree. He hacked and chopped away at the tree as chips gave way, little by little. As he focused on the V-shaped impression, he was about midway through the girth of the tree when he had a decision to make: either give the tree one more swing of the ax, which would cause it to topple over, or he could put down the ax and walk away. He could not explain why, but he decided to walk away, and it was at that moment he came out of the coma.

Dad eventually recovered and was transported to Walter Reed National Naval Medical Center (now the Walter Reed National Military Medical Center) in Washington, D.C. Sergeant Spencer insisted and indeed fought to remain in the Army even with the loss of his left hand. He loved the Army and could not imagine himself returning to the farm. To prove his worth he voluntarily took an expert marksman test to demonstrate that he could still handle a rifle, and he passed with flying colors. With passing scores in hand, his company first sergeant allowed Dad to re-enlist and assigned him to Forest Glen Annex in Washington, D.C., to work on future prosthetics technology for the remainder of his Army career.

I was stunned by this revelation but grateful that although he previously could not muster the words to tell me about his war injury, at least I now understood what happened. As I renewed the oath of office during my colonel promotion ceremony, I could not get the thoughts of his horrific experience out of my mind. A few years later, at the age of eighty, Dad finally sought help for the stress and horror of that experience. The term "post-traumatic stress disorder" was not used in the early 1950s, and unfortunately Dad and many others like him carried those wounds of war with them for a lifetime.

But, There Are No Golf Courses in Southeast D.C.!!!

On a warm Saturday morning in September 1996, I woke up earlier than usual for a weekend. The temperatures were unseasonably warm, and following a hectic first week on the new job at Tinker AFB, Oklahoma, I wanted to take a relaxing run before the temperatures got too hot. Tinker AFB is one of the largest installations in the Air Force and has a long, scenic jogging path through trees, past ponds, and with an abundance of wildlife to observe along the way. I could feel the stress of the week melt away as I completed my run and stepped inside the house. So when Ora informed me that the commander of the Oklahoma City Air Logistics Center, Maj. Gen. Carlos Perez, had called, there was no reason for alarm. Rather than return the call immediately, I took a shower, had some breakfast, and settled in to my rocking chair on the back patio before I gave the general a return call.

"Larry," exclaimed General Perez. "What the hell took you so long to return my call? I'm on YOUR golf course and it looks like crap. The greens are not properly manicured and the water on several holes is hot. I know you just arrived but as the support group commander this is YOUR responsibility, and I expect YOU to fix it. Is that clear?"

"Yes, sir," I responded as I felt my stress level go from -5 to 10 in less than a minute. Having been raised on the Horseshoe, I had never seen a golf course, much less played the game. After being chewed out by my new boss, though, I had to learn, and learn fast.

First thing Monday morning, I met with my civilian director for morale, welfare, and recreation (MWR), who happened to be a scratch golfer. Care and maintenance of the golf course fell squarely in his job description. He apologized profusely for my weekend butt chewing and said he would take care of the problem immediately. I told him I could not afford another episode like that with the commander, so we would both take care of the problem. But first, I asked him for a favor: to teach me how to play golf. After a quick lesson on the driving range, we scheduled tee times for every Saturday morning, quite intentionally about twenty minutes ahead of Major General Perez and his group.

I must admit that we were quite a sight driving a golf cart loaded down with weed eaters, buckets of ice, and trash bags to ensure the course was in top shape as the general traversed the course behind us. As the fall season came to a close, the cold weather suspended the general's Saturday golf outings, so I got a break until spring. I actually developed into a fair golfer, and, more importantly, I never got chewed out about the conditions of the course again. That said, despite the initial harsh reprimand I received, Major General Perez was actually a great boss who taught me a great deal about how to be a commander, including the fine art of butt chewing when necessary.

Joan Orr Air Force Spouse of the Year

My immediate boss was Col. Robert "Bob" Smolen. Bob was a tremendous leader and became a great mentor and friend. Bob had unlimited energy, and he made coming to work every day a joy.

Should they choose to do so, spouses can play a significant role with the day-to-day family support of a military unit. Ora is not the type of person that seeks the limelight, instead preferring to work behind the scenes and let others take the credit. Even so, her quiet yet significant contributions on Tinker were noticed by just about everyone. She could be found pulling up weeds in flower beds to picking up trash off the street. She worked tirelessly with family support programs and was a fixture in the Child Development Center. In particular, Major General Perez and Colonel Smolen noticed Ora's hard work and approached me about submitting her for the Joan Orr Air Force Spouse of the Year award.

The Joan Orr Award is highly prestigious and recognizes contributions to the U.S. Air Force community by nonmilitary spouses of Air Force service members. The award honors the late Mrs. Joan Orr, wife of Verne Orr, former Secretary of the Air Force. Nomination packages are based on accomplishments of an individual's specific contributions to the Air Force community in specific areas such as base and community activities, Air Force–related organizations, demonstration of leadership, and membership in professional, civil, and cultural organizations.

Ora vigorously protested. She insisted she did not want any credit for doing something she loved. She was happy to support Air Force families and was committed to supporting me as their commander, but being recognized for that support was out of the question. Unfortunately for me, my bosses would not take no for an answer, so I craftily imparted bits and pieces of information from Ora each day about the activities she was involved in until I had just enough information to write up the award, which she won. As a result, her name is permanently etched on a plaque displayed in the Pentagon. The downside is that after her selection, I was known around the base as "Ora's husband."

Fighting against Inefficiency

When given the unique opportunity to become the Mission Support Group commander, my passion for efficiency and cost savings continued to accelerate. Tinker AFB is a large installation with a rough circumference of fifteen miles, which is three to four times the size of most Air Force installations. The reason I am so familiar with the distance is occasionally another mentor, then Brig. Gen. Don Wetekam, who was a very good distance runner (Don went on to be promoted to lieutenant general), would drag me kicking and screaming for a jog around the base. It was during one of those runs that I noticed a large blue government bus traversing the perimeter, and it appeared to be mostly empty.

My curiosity drove me to hitch a ride on the bus to observe the ridership. After riding the base perimeter several times I got to know the bus driver pretty well, because he and I were the only passengers. I asked him if the low passenger volume bothered him. His reply was that "if the government is willing to pay me to drive an empty bus, I will happily accept their money to do so." I dug further by checking the dispatch office for the base taxi, which consisted of a fleet of cars that were on call for those needing more individual transportation assistance.

When I reviewed the dispatch requests I was shocked to discover the predominant ridership fell into two categories: First were airmen residing in the dormitories who requested personal rides to and from work and to the dining facility. Second were employees with revoked driving privileges, primarily due to driving under the influence. In the latter case, employees drove their private vehicles to a parking lot just outside the base and used the base taxi to traverse the base during the workday. Clearly the base taxi was not intended for these purposes, so we discontinued the inappropriate use and revamped the bus service.

Another expense that bothered me was the base library. I have nothing against libraries, but a survey showed that 90 percent of the regular attendees were retirees. I also have nothing against retirees, but this seemed like a high price to pay for occasional usage. Coincidentally, a local college had a library just outside the base entry gate that was exponentially better equipped and was open longer hours. So I visited the college library and secured an agreement to provide library cards to military members, including military dependents and retirees. This was great news, and Colonel Smolen agreed with my recommendation to close the base library.

Unfortunately the closure was short-lived. In many ways, Colonel Smolen and I were ahead of our time. Whereas today many libraries and bookstores have closed, that was not the case during my time at Tinker. So when a commander on Tinker who was assigned to a different command complained, we were directed to reopen the library. We were also ahead of our time on another cost-saving proposal that went all the way to the Pentagon. At the time, my son Derrick was in college at East Carolina University. When I visited him, I noticed his meal plan allowed him to dine at several eateries around the campus. In the Air Force, a meal card is accepted only at the base dining facility, even though food options are provided at base clubs, the bowling alley, the golf course, and so on. It seemed to me that airmen ought to get the same options Derrick had at college.

We surveyed the base dining facility and were again surprised by the results. Most of the people who frequented the dining facility were more senior in rank and did not possess meal cards. In essence, they were taking advantage of the reduced prices for breakfast and lunch. Ironically, those junior airmen the dining facility was designed to support consumed an average of less than one meal a day. We knew it would be viewed as a radical idea, but we suggested that the base dining facility be closed and those with meal cards be allowed to eat at any one of the many facilities that served food on the base. As an added bonus, the proposal would increase revenues for MWR facilities that served meals. My bosses loved the idea, so we wrote a letter to our four-star commander at Air Force Materiel Command (AFMC) for his support, and he concurred. Since this proposal would set a new precedent for the Air Force, the AFMC commander endorsed the memorandum to the Pentagon for approval.

Unfortunately, during the legal review it was discovered that the Tinker dining facility contract employed people with disabilities, so we could not break the contract. I completely understood this but argued the Air Force should seek dining facilities without the disability stipulation and implement the idea at other bases where it made sense. This idea, however, was viewed as too radical and was discarded. Again, in hindsight we were ahead of the curve because today many bases have closed dining facilities and replaced them with more economical alternatives. Despite the legal ruling, we were not deterred. We went on to close an auxiliary dining facility as well as implement many other efficiency initiatives. We also convinced our headquarters to establish a cost savings web page so bases across the Air Force could have access to cost-saving opportunities from a central repository.

You Can't Park There!

At most Air Force facilities, certain high-volume locations such as the commissary, the base exchange store, and the gymnasium have reserved parking for senior officers and enlisted members. This benefit is not so much about "rank has its privileges" as it is about acknowledging the busy schedule of commanders and senior noncommissioned officers. On a busy Saturday morning, Ora and I pulled into the reserved colonel parking space at the commissary. I was in civilian clothes because we were hosting a large social gathering at our home for members of my group and were doing some last-minute shopping.

As we exited the car, two gentlemen approached us, and one of them asked why we were violating base regulations by parking in a spot we were not entitled to. When I assured them I was authorized to park in the space, one of the gentlemen demanded to see my identification card. Everything that was within me said I should tell this joker where to get off, but I didn't. I calmly showed him my ID while simultaneously pointing out the colonel eagle insignia on my car windshield. Faced with this nonrefutable evidence, they both left in a huff, but not before commenting something to the effect that the Air Force must be desperate to promote a black man to colonel.

About midway through my Mission Support Group tour, I visited the Pentagon to get advice on my next assignment. I met with a major general in charge of personnel assignments. Based on my record of performance and command experience, he suggested that I consider a military assistant job to a senior Air Force or senior civilian in the Office of the Secretary of Defense. My initial reaction was that I'd be thrilled to have such a position, and I offered the possibility of military assistant to the Secretary of the Air Force (SECAF). Coincidentally, the rumored new incoming SECAF was an African American. The major general bristled at the suggestion and counseled me that it would not look right for a black senior leader to hire a black assistant. As a colonel, I swallowed hard and responded to this major general that white senior officials routinely hire white military assistants and no one complains. His only retort was, "That's different."

I Know You Are My Boss, But . . . !

As my two-year command tour was coming to an end, Major General Perez called me into his office. He knew the Air Force would want me to return to the financial management career field, but he thought I had more to offer. Specifically, Perez knew that I was eligible to compete for wing command, so he got right to the point. "Larry, I am very happy with your performance here at Tinker, but you are very young to become a wing commander. So, although you are technically eligible to compete now, I recommend you take your name out of competition, and I want you to stay at Tinker and work for me in the logistics center."

I responded, "Sir, I very much appreciate your counsel. I know you are looking out for my best interest. However, even though I am really junior, wing command is the ultimate leadership opportunity, and I hate to take myself out of the running."

A bit agitated by my response, Perez said, "Look, Larry, I'm a major general. I know what's best for you. You need to stay here and learn about the logistics business. That will prepare you for broader opportunities in the future. Is that understood?"

"Yes, sir," I responded. "I appreciate your support, and I'll do whatever the Air Force needs me to do."

Following that advice, I consulted with several of my mentors, including my wing commander. To a person, all agreed I should never take myself out of competition for wing command. Even if selected, I could always decline, but self-elimination was out of the question. With that advice, and with the unlikely chance of selection, I remained eligible. A month or so later, while attending a base social function in the Officer's Club, Perez literally grabbed me by the arm and said he had just returned as a member of the wing command selection board! Talk about an OMG moment! Before I could respond, he told me I was on the wing commander list.

He reminded me of our earlier conversation and said he was disappointed by my defiance. But he went on to say he had been granted the option of removing my name from the list but decided against doing so. He agreed that wing command was a unique privilege and offered congratulations for my selection. He then offered to do whatever he could to ensure I got that opportunity. With less than eighteen years of commissioned service, I was the most junior colonel to be selected for wing command, but Perez kept his word. After several phone calls and personal recommendations, Perez confirmed my selection as the next wing commander at Hill AFB, Utah. As I prepared to depart Tinker AFB, I was eternally grateful to Brig. Gen. Si Johnson for bringing me to Tinker and to Maj. Gen. Carlos Perez and Col. Bob Smolen for their unyielding support, leadership, and mentorship.

Wing Command

In February 2000, I was honored to take over the leadership reins of the 75th Air Base Wing, Hill AFB, Utah. Wing command is what every officer dreams of. It is an opportunity to lead an entire base installation. Colonels (O-6) command most wings, which include four subordinate groups: Operations Group, Mission Support Group, Medical Group, and Logistics Group, all of which are also commanded by colonels. Wing command is the ultimate leadership opportunity and can range in size from three thousand personnel to more than six thousand.

Little did I know that this job, at this time, would be my toughest career leadership challenge to date. The incumbent commander had been relieved of duty, so when I arrived, the wing was without a commander and was in some turmoil, and morale was low. Most critically, I arrived with a major operational readiness inspection (ORI) scheduled in sixty days. To make matters worse, the base had just failed a practice inspection. From the moment I assumed command, I was completely consumed with getting the base ready for inspection. My family and I drove onto Hill AFB in February 2000, and I don't think we drove off base until the ORI was concluded in April.

For a wing commander, an ORI is serious business. An ORI is the ultimate test of a unit's readiness to perform its wartime mission. Failures have oftentimes resulted in the firing of the wing commander. The base had not had a major inspection in five years, and it showed. My initial assessment was that we would fail the ORI unless we took drastic measures to get ready in a hurry. To start, we scheduled a series of mass briefings in the base movie theater, which allowed me to personally speak with all ten thousand employees. This not only included those in my wing but also those assigned to the Ogden Air Logistics Center, who are mostly civilian and would be critical to our success. We explained the importance of the ORI and, more importantly, that our very reason for being was to be ready for war and that the ORI would test our ability to be ready. We trained day and night for two months straight and everyone was exhausted; but come inspection time, we felt prepared.

The inspection team hit with a fury. Since I had been part of the ORI during my previous assignment at Tinker, they were especially tough on us. In a highly unusual move, they hit us with a simulated kidnapping of the Air Logistics Center commander and his deputy, while simultaneously simulating a base gate "runner," which is someone speeding through the base gate without authorization. To add realism, they actually brought a crashed vehicle on base to simulate a major accident. As we quickly gathered the base leadership together, the thought occurred that we should separate each incident to better multitask the response. Despite the added complexity, the members of the wing performed magnificently, and we calmly solved each challenge effectively and efficiently.

After an intense first two days, I departed my home on base as usual to walk to my office. Immediately, two menacing-looking men approached me and said, "Exercise, exercise, exercise; we are kidnapping and detaining you." They actually blindfolded me and took me to a room in our base billeting office. They explained I was temporarily being taken out of the exercise to test my deputy commander. Once in the room, they asked if I would like breakfast. I responded affirmatively and gave them my order. When the two inspectors departed the room, I grabbed my belongings, climbed out the window of the first floor room, and went to work. The chief inspector was furious, but he could not complain since I responded exactly like I would have had the situation been real.

The Air Force has three Air Logistics Centers (ALCs), and up to that point no ALC had been graded above satisfactory. So when it was announced that we had received the first excellent score, the exhilaration on Hill AFB was pure ecstasy! The inspector general report read in part, "Best commander involvement ever seen," "excelled during our toughest scenario given to date." Following the inspection the base celebrated with a base picnic. The inspection preparation and results had united more than ten thousand employees unlike anything I had ever witnessed. I had always believed that leadership could transform an organization, and we were privileged to witness that firsthand.

Following the ORI, we were called upon to respond to a real-time emergency contingency, Operation Desert Thunder/Fox. Desert Thunder was in response to threats by Iraq's president Saddam Hussein to shoot down U-2 spy planes in violation of the no-fly zone. Desert Fox involved a major four-day bombing campaign on Iraqi targets due to Iraq's failure to comply with United Nations (UN) Security Council resolutions and its interference with UN Special Commission inspectors.

The preparation and loading of large cargo planes with equipment, munitions, and spare parts was grueling, but the opportunity to support a real wartime mission sent the morale on base sky high. Late one night, the 388th Fighter Wing commander, Col. Mike Hostage, who went on to become a four-star general, and I met on the flight line to watch a squadron of his F-16s take off to their overseas location. I literally got goose bumps as I witnessed rings of fire against the dark night sky as the F-16s took off in afterburner. Fortunately, tensions subsided and our troops and equipment returned safely. But I will never forget the charge we felt knowing our country asked us to go to war and we responded.

A year and a half into my tour, my boss received a call from the Pentagon. The senior financial manager in charge of assignments wanted me back into the career field. The job being considered was budget director at a major command. Since I was a wing commander, my boss felt this was at best a lateral assignment, and he protested for a bigger job. At one point, our four-star senior commander of Air Force Materiel Command engaged and got my new assignment upgraded to comptroller for Air Combat Command (ACC), the largest command in the Air Force. Although I had nothing to do with this resolution, rumor had it that the head financial management major general thought ill of me because what appeared to be an "end run." If he was concerned about the change in assignment, however, he never mentioned it, and about the time I was due to report to my new job, he retired from the Air Force.

The awards garnered by the 75th Air Base Wing are too numerous to list. During my change of command ceremony I looked out over the wing members and could not have been prouder. Whenever we had a challenge, they stepped forward and performed brilliantly. I was also proud of my wife Ora and daughter Shannon. There is no playbook to explain the demands of a wing commander's spouse, but Ora put at least as much effort into the wing as I did. Likewise, living in Utah, Shannon was thrust into a completely unfamiliar environment and culture but never once complained. With wing command behind me, we set off for the cross-country drive to Langley AFB, Virginia, where I would preside over the financial affairs of a war-fighting command during periods of peace and war.

9/11

Tuesday, September 11, 2001, was a beautiful day in Hampton, Virginia. I was at work when I heard talk that an airplane had crashed into one of the World Trade Center's Twin Towers in New York City. My immediate reaction was that it had to be a terrible accident . . . until the second airplane rammed the other tower. At that point, we all knew something was wrong. When yet another airplane hit the Pentagon there was no doubt. We were under attack. So the base immediately went into emergency operations. As a nation and as a military, we were clearly not prepared for an aerial attack of this nature. The 1st Fighter Wing at Langley was home to F-15C fighter aircraft. Without being told to do so, they quickly recovered the aircraft that were flying and started to prepare for whatever orders might come.

Saturday, September 15, 2001, would normally be a day off, but our headquarters was in full contingency preparation. Following a commanders' staff meeting, I decided to take a quick run along the base jogging trail. About one mile into my run, I noticed something up ahead on the path that appeared to be someone lying on the ground. As I got closer, it was indeed a gentleman who appeared to be unconscious. As I stopped to assess the situation, quite by chance a nurse that was also jogging approached the scene. She immediately began CPR as I raced to the nearest on-base home and called an ambulance. Unfortunately, the master sergeant, who had just recently relocated to the base, passed away. I felt horrible for his family. As I was detailing the incident at the base hospital, I received a phone call to return to work.

Initial planning for Operation Enduring Freedom (OEF) and subsequently Operation Iraqi Freedom (OIF) was well under way. As the senior financial officer for the command, it was my responsibility to rally the troops to the call. Money and war are inextricably linked. In 415 BC, during a speech to the Syracusans, Hermocrates said, "They [the Athenians] have abundance of gold and silver and these make war, like other things, go smoothly."[3] From funding war operations to ensuring troop pay to deploying hundreds of "finance" airmen to the theater of operations, this war, like my first, used every inch of my strength and experience.

Once again, the folks assigned to the Air Combat Command Comptroller Directorate performed brilliantly. In particular, my civilian deputy director of budget, Ms. Patricia Carey, was magnificent. Pat was smart, dedicated, and as hardworking as they come. Through the ups and downs of financial management during both peace and war, Pat was the glue that held the command office together.

Another talented person on the staff was Mrs. Gladys Henderson-Williams. Gladys was an expert on the technical aspects of accounting and was an absolute pleasure to work with. In addition to her technical skill, Gladys served as our unofficial chaplain and counselor.

Gladys possesses a rare quality of identifying with people and gaining their trust and confidence. If someone on the staff had a problem, they called on Gladys. If someone had marital trouble, they called Gladys. If someone was frustrated and needed a listening ear, they went to Gladys. Most of all, if someone needed prayer, they went to Gladys. In today's politically correct environment, praying for a co-worker on duty is discouraged. Fortunately for me, our staff had such confidence in Gladys that political correctness took a back seat. She was one of the true leaders on the staff.

What, Me, a General Officer?

I had never put much thought behind becoming a general officer. I suppose my own unconscious bias was partly to blame, but I simply could not envision myself at that grade. Even so, I believed then and I still believe that "blooming where you are planted" is the best career advice I ever received. Besides, selection to general officer is so rare that contemplating such an accomplishment is wasted effort. As a colonel and senior financial manager for ACC, I knew there were only two brigadier general positions for financial managers in the entire Air Force, but I was not presumptuous enough to believe I could be one of those two. In retrospect, though, that I had been the only financial manager to command a wing and that I had been promoted six years ahead of my peers should have made me more optimistic.

I arrived at Langley AFB as a junior colonel, and I remained on the ACC staff for four years, even though previous tour lengths for my predecessors were two years. I was in the most challenging financial job in the Air Force, so to reassign me simply based on tenure was not sensible. During my third year, I received my promotion recommendation form that made it clear my boss was pushing for my promotion. It was a bit early to be promoted to one-star, but the words on my form were undeniable. I was rated near the top of all eligible colonels in the command and number one of ten colonels on the ACC staff. The ACC commander and my boss was Gen. Hal Hornburg. This was the same Hal Hornburg I had worked for when he was the wing commander at Seymour Johnson AFB who got me promoted below the zone to lieutenant colonel.

General Hornburg was and remains a mentor and friend. The style, class, and professionalism he and his wife Cynthia modeled as wing commander at Seymour Johnson AFB, particularly during Operation Desert Shield/Storm, were impeccable. I had all but forgotten about the potential promotion until late one day following a routine staff meeting, General Hornburg asked me to step inside his office. As he closed the door behind me, he informed me I had been selected for brigadier general. I don't think General Hornburg noticed, but as he spoke those words, I became anesthetized. This was a pinch-me moment. Achieving general officer rank comes with a special trust and makes one immediately recognizable. It was a conversation in my life that I will never forget.

Shortly after that meeting I received a call from Gen. Lester Lyles, commander of Air Force Materiel Command. Lyles was a bright and impressive general officer who had mentored me as a young officer. As a four-star general, Lyles was rare. As a black four-star general who was not a pilot, he was the rarest of the rare. A visionary leader, Lyles created a new directorate that streamlined headquarters operations. This new Directorate of Mission Support consolidated all base support functions under the leadership of one person. Although it would be several months before I actually pinned on the new rank, Lyles selected me to stand up this new directorate at Wright-Patterson AFB, Ohio.

7

RAREFIED AIR

Rank does not confer privilege or give power.
It imposes responsibility.

—PETER DRUCKER[1]

en. Colin Powell, former Chairman of the Joint Chiefs of Staff and Secretary of State, tells a story about brigadier generals. During the height of
the Civil War, President Abraham Lincoln enjoyed taking a walk to the northern
part of the city to relax. During one of those walks, he visited the Old Soldiers'
Home, which happened to contain a telegraph station. While there, an important telegraph arrived from Manassas, Virginia, which the president read. A Union
encampment had been attacked by the Confederacy, resulting in the capture of
one hundred horses and a brigadier general. The president turned to the telegraph
operator and lamented over the loss of horses. The telegraph operator was a bit
surprised and asked the president if he was at all concerned about the brigadier
general. President Lincoln replied that he could make another brigadier general in
five minutes, but it would be extremely difficult to replace one hundred horses![2]

On July 1, 2004, President Lincoln's view notwithstanding, I became a brigadier general. I adjusted my uniform and straightened my tie as I stood in front of
the bathroom mirror in the basement of my parents' home. In doing so, I could not
help but gaze at the colonel rank on the shoulder of my uniform shirt. I had worn
that rank since January 1998, and it had become a part of who I was. Outside
of my family, for six years I had been known to most as Colonel Spencer, but on

this day in 2004 that would change. Rather than have the ceremony conducted at my home station at Wright-Patterson AFB in Ohio, I reserved a room at the Bolling AFB, Officer's Club so my relatives and friends could attend. My former wing commander from Tinker AFB, now Maj. Gen. Robert "Bob" Smolen, agreed to officiate the ceremony.

Smolen and I stood outside the room where the ceremony would be held. On cue, we stepped smartly into the room and walked down the aisle toward the front as the proffer requested that everyone please rise from their seats. As we reached the front of the room, the proffer announced, "Post the Colors" as the Air Force Honor Guard marched forward with flags in preparation for the national anthem. Following the anthem, everyone took their seats as Major General Smolen spoke about about my career and the promotion ceremony. Following Smolen's comments, I was called to center stage, where he and Ora pinned on my new rank, making me the newest Air Force brigadier general.

Following the ceremony, Ora and I immediately drove back to Wright-Patterson AFB, which is one of the largest and most diverse and complex installations in the Air Force. Its heritage ties directly to Wilbur Wright Field, which was established in 1917. Standing up a new group of disparate support functions was the type of challenge I thrived on. Unfortunately, General Lyles retired shortly after my arrival. But our new commander, Gen. Gregory "Speedy" Martin, was an exceptional leader and a thrill to work for. Witnessing General Martin corral his new command and take it to heights previously unimaginable was a leadership laboratory. Martin possessed unlimited energy, stamina, and an unquenchable thirst for excellence. I immediately took to his leadership style and "adopted" him as a mentor who also became a friend and confidant. Before long, Martin had established Air Force Materiel Command as a force to be reckoned with.

Leading the newly created Mission Support Directorate was a unique opportunity. My task was to mold five previously independent functions into one synergistic group to develop policy and direction for thousands of support functions throughout the command. One of my first tasks was to select a deputy, and I was indeed fortunate to have Col. Linda Jones as my second-in-command. Linda and I had previously been stationed together as majors at Seymour Johnson AFB in the early 1990s, and she was a sharp and supportive partner. Together, Linda and I led the new directorate to such success that the Air Force adopted our model as a template for the entire Air Force.

After working for General Martin for about eighteen months, he called me into his office for career counseling. He expressed that my potential was bigger than the financial management career field, so he wanted to broaden my experience base. He decided to reassign me to Tinker AFB in Oklahoma, but this time as the vice commander of the Air Logistics Center. This would be a unique opportunity to revel in my love of airplanes and use my academic training in industrial engineering. I thoroughly enjoyed my time at Wright-Patterson and was proud of standing up a new unit, but the opportunity to help lead depot operations for some of the world's most lethal aircraft was a dream come true.

Leading Depot Operations

I was excited as I drove through the front gate of Tinker AFB again. The Oklahoma City Air Logistics Center (OC-ALC) is an amazing installation with a huge mission. They are responsible for depot operations for the B-52, B-1, B-2, KC-135, and E-3 (AWACS) aircraft; expanded phase maintenance on the Navy E-6 aircraft; and maintenance, repair, and overhaul of several high-performance aircraft engines. Additionally, the complex is responsible for the maintenance, repair, and overhaul of a myriad of Air Force and Navy airborne accessory components. The OC-ALC employs more than 9,400 military and civilian personnel with ninety-eight different job skills. The large complex has sixty-three buildings and 8.2 million square feet of industrial floor space and is the largest employer in Oklahoma.

I had the pleasure of working for Mr. Robert (Bob) Connor. Bob made history as the first civilian to lead an Air Force Logistics Center. Bob was smart, a strong leader, and did a magnificent job running the center. My office was in a one-square-mile building, where each day I witnessed rows and rows of airplanes stripped down to the metal. Thousands of dedicated civilian and military employees moved smartly about the building preparing aircraft and parts for return to service. From run-testing newly repaired jet engines to crawling through the bowels of a B-52 bomber aircraft, I literally did not want to leave at the end of each workday. In fact, I often visited our aircraft mechanics repairing aircraft on weekends and holidays.

I was "living my dream" at Tinker when General Martin announced his retirement. This news brought some concern, since he was the one who had fought back attempts by my career field managers to bring me back into financial management. But once his retirement was final, I no longer had his shield of protection, and I was quickly put on assignment back to the Pentagon to work in financial management. Since I had been assigned to Tinker for less than a year, I petitioned to remain at least another twelve months. But that petition fell on deaf ears, and I was directed to report to the Pentagon as the director of budget operations (Financial Management Budget Office) for the Air Force.

Back to the Pentagon

When I returned to the D.C. area in the summer of 2006, I found the Pentagon to be a much different place than it had been in the early 1980s. Computers had replaced many of the previous manual tasks. To avoid the commuting nightmare associated with a D.C. assignment, I elected to move into base housing at Bolling AFB, which is only a short six miles away. Working in budget in the Pentagon can be difficult work, but I enjoyed it. Just as I began to hit my stride, I was informed I had been selected for promotion to major general, news that was met with both elation and relief.

There is only one financial management major general position in the entire Air Force, the director of budget (FMB), so I was relieved that my boss, Maj. Gen. Frank Faykes, an extraordinary leader, occupied that position and was not due for a move. So I assumed (hoped) I would be reassigned to a new job outside the Pentagon soon and back to a field unit, which I most enjoyed. While waiting for news on my next assignment, Faykes suddenly and surprisingly announced his retirement. Adding to the surprise, Faykes confided he had recommended me as his replacement. Up to that point in Air Force history, no African American had ever reached the top budget job for the Air Force. Despite my desires to the contrary, I would be the first.

Leading FMB was a great leadership challenge. It was effectively three jobs in one. First, we worked with the Air Force Major Commands in the daily execution of their programs, ensuring that Air Force operations and readiness remained on track. Second, we worked the daily grind and demands of the Pentagon in support of the Planning, Programming, Budget, and Execution system. This involved the annual execution of the budget as well as the five-year defense program. Finally, I was responsible as a congressional liaison for the Appropriations Committees. This meant frequent visits to Capitol Hill and preparing the Secretary of the Air Force and chief of staff for congressional budget hearings and testimony.

Historically, one avoided an assignment to FMB in the Pentagon at all costs. It had a reputation as a sweatshop, and legend has it that the office actually stored sleeping cots so analysts could spend the night when things got really busy. In my view, this reputation was largely self-inflicted and unnecessary. So we took it as a personal challenge to make FMB a fun and desirable place to work. Before I departed, word had spread that FMB was no longer a dreaded assignment. Rather, we had officers and enlisted members in the field actually fighting for an assignment to the Pentagon. Even though this was not the job I would have chosen, I was proud of what the staff accomplished. In addition to justifying and executing billions of dollars for Air Force Operations, we transformed the work environment in FMB from one of dread to one with more work-life balance.

Rest in Peace Old Sarge

At the end of September 2008, I was relieved that we had successfully concluded another fiscal year. But we were about to gear up to deliver the next fiscal year's budget, so we were extremely busy. While working late one evening in October, Ora called and said Dad wanted my siblings and me to accompany him to a doctor's appointment at Walter Reed. This was extremely unusual because neither of my parents ever discussed their medical issues. Much to our surprise, we discovered that Dad had previously been diagnosed with lesions on his pancreas that were now increasing in number and size. While there had been no firm diagnosis of cancer, Dad was convinced the disease was inevitable.

The Army surgeon explained that the only treatment was a complicated surgery called a "whipple" procedure, which would remove a portion of his pancreas, bile duct, small intestine, and stomach. Dad was eighty-one years of age, and the surgeon warned him that a procedure of this magnitude would be hard on him, and he was particularly concerned whether Dad's body could withstand the difficult recovery. Whereas my siblings and I were skeptical, Dad was more pragmatic. To him, the decision was black and white. He did not want to risk a cancer diagnosis and the associated surgery and chemotherapy. He was resigned to rolling the dice, fully recognizing it could end his life. At Dad's insistence, the surgeon agreed to perform the surgery.

The surgery was scheduled in January 2009. Early on the day of the surgery I braved the Washington, D.C., traffic to Walter Reed. I was in uniform, fully expecting to return to work after the scheduled two- to three-hour surgery. When I arrived, Dad was already being prepped. I walked back to the preparation area to see him before the anesthesia was administered. The pastor of his church was by his side. When the pastor departed, I had a few minutes alone with him. He told me how proud he was of me. His family was steeped in military tradition and service, but none had become commissioned officers, much less a general officer. He said he was not sure how the surgery would turn out, but he was prepared either way. Dad had been raised not to show emotion, and he raised his children the same way. As he spoke, however, I felt a lump in my throat as he told me he was prepared to die.

As I was his oldest child, he said he was not worried about our family because he knew I would step in to keep everyone together. He was the family patriarch, and in his own way he asked me to assume that role if the surgery did not go well. As the medical attendants wheeled him away, I was struck by how at peace he appeared. He knew the odds of the surgery and was completely comfortable with his decision. Once the surgery started, what we had been told would be a two- or three-hour procedure lasted about eight hours. After the surgery, the surgeon greeted us in the waiting room and said Dad had come through reasonably well, but it had been difficult. He also reiterated that at his age, recovery would be long and challenging. When we visited him in the intensive care unit (ICU) he was unconscious. Seeing him that way was difficult, but the hardest part was over. At least that's what we assumed.

What followed was a roller coaster of improvement one day, followed by a setback the next. He spent an inordinate amount of time in the ICU before he was moved to a recovery ward. Regardless, the roller coaster continued. One day we were encouraged, only to hear the following day that he had contracted one infection or another. We could see that he was fighting for his life, but his immune system was struggling to keep up. At one critical point, he suffered a seizure, followed by a heart stoppage.

Mom was in the room at the time and was traumatized by the episode. I received a phone call to rush to the hospital because it was apparent he would not survive. When I arrived, the medical team had restarted his heart but said he had most certainly suffered brain damage. This prognosis prompted the hospital staff to meet with our family to discuss final plans. Specifically, they thought we should seriously consider signing a do not resuscitate (DNR) authorization and discontinuing the assisted breathing apparatus.

We agreed to the DNR but declined to discontinue the ventilator. We had seen him bounce back too many times to not give him a fighting chance. Much to the surprise of his attending physicians, fight back he did. Adding to the surprise, we received confirmation that he had suffered no brain damage as a result of the heart stoppage. This up-and-down pattern continued until he finally settled into a state of limbo where he was neither getting worse nor better, so he was transferred to a rehabilitation center in Washington, D.C. During his short stay, he was essentially nonresponsive and soon began to decline.

On Memorial Day 2009, I visited him alone in his room. I had struggled with my prayers for his recovery. On the one hand, I prayed for him to recover. I just wanted things to go back to the way they were. On the other hand, I wondered if that was selfish on my part. He had lived a full and happy life and maybe it was time for us to let go. I knew that if he could speak, he would not want to remain in his current state. In his room that Memorial Day, with just the two of us, I simply prayed that God's will be done and went home. Less than twelve hours later, I got a call from the rehab center informing me that he had passed away.

Since we had been raised to suppress emotion, following the funeral I buried myself in work. Just one day following the burial I was in front of a roomful of cameras and press people, briefing them on the Air Force's new fiscal year's budget. In prior years I had conducted the budget briefing alone, but this time I asked my talented deputy, Pat Zarodkiewicz, to stand with me. I'm not sure why I needed Pat, but I did. During the drive home that day, the finality of Dad's death hit me. Despite the funeral and burial services, suddenly the reality that Dad was gone became real.

During the heavy rush hour traffic, I pulled my car over to the side of the road on Interstate 295 and sat there for a few minutes. I was oblivious to where I was or what I was doing. Suddenly a driver pulled up beside me, blew his horn, and asked if I was okay. I responded that I was fine and thanked him. With that brief inter-action, I was back to reality. I pulled back onto the highway and continued my drive home with the reassurance that although he was no longer with us, Dad had lived a good life and was now in a better place. I also reminded myself that one day we would see each other again.

A Third Star!

Things were going well as I led the Air Force budget office, but since my predecessors had retired from that job, I assumed I would eventually do the same. Besides, no career financial manager had ever been promoted above the two-star rank, so I was extremely grateful to have reached that pinnacle. Then, following a routine meeting, the Air Force chief of staff, Gen. Norty Schwartz, asked me to step into his office. General Schwartz informed me that the office of the director for Force Structure, Resources, and Assessments (J-8) on the Joint Staff, a lieutenant general billet, would soon be vacant and he wanted to nominate me for the job. I was floored by this news but also honored and grateful that he thought so highly of my potential. Since I was a relative unknown in the Joint Staff world, I was scheduled for interviews with the director of the Joint Staff, Lt. Gen. Stanley McChrystal, the vice chairman of the Joint Chiefs of Staff, Gen. James (Hoss) Cartwright, and the chairman of the Joint Chiefs of Staff, Adm. Michael Mullen.

I felt good about the interviews but had no idea how I had done or who my competitors were. By far the most intriguing interview was with Admiral Mullen. I had seen him on the Sunday talk shows but had never actually met him. I found him to be engaging and smart, and he was clearly carrying a huge responsibility on his shoulders. He asked penetrating questions and listened intently as I responded. I gave it my best shot, but I figured that with no previous joint experience, I was at best a long shot for the job. However, hearing Admiral Mullen talk about the responsibilities he shouldered, I walked away from the interview grateful that he was leading our military.

A month or so passed without a whisper about the new job. In this case, I assumed no news was bad news, but having risen to the top spot in my career field, I certainly had no reason to complain. During a visit to Capitol Hill with General Schwartz, we entered a small room so I could update him about the details of the visit. At one point, General Schwartz abruptly interrupted and congratulated me on my selection as the next J-8 on the Joint Staff. I barely maintained my composure as we departed the small office to visit a member of the Senate. In addition to the promotion to lieutenant general, I was actually more excited to work directly for the chairman of the Joint Chiefs of Staff (CJCS). General Schwartz smiled and gave me one bit of advice about the new job: Don't "F" it up! I assured him I would not! On my first day in the new office, I noticed a picture wall of previous J-8s dating back decades. Once again, I noticed I would be the first African American to hold the job.

The J-8 job was as exhilarating as it was challenging. The hours were long and the demands were heavy, but the work was exciting and fun. I often found myself in a senior leader meeting led by the secretary of defense, service chiefs, and combatant commanders. As the Air Force budget director, I briefed their budget each year. As the J-8, the OSD comptroller and I would now brief the entire DoD budget to the press and on Capitol Hill. For the first time in my career, I had a bird's-eye view of the entire Department of Defense. My job on the Joint Staff was to be "purple"—that is, to represent all of the DoD, not just the Air Force. If there was ever a job I felt I had prepared for my entire career, the J-8 was it.

The tour length on the Joint Staff was generally two years. So once I completed eighteen months on the job, I began thinking about retirement. When I discussed my plans with the chairman, he asked if I would remain for a third year. With a great job, great boss, and the best deputy I could have hoped for in Ms. Lisa Disbrow, I was happy to remain for an additional year. A month later, I got a call from General Schwartz. This time he informed me that he planned to nominate me for promotion to four-star general and to serve as the thirty-seventh vice chief of staff of the Air Force. No one with my background as a financial manager had ever been promoted to three stars, much less to four. I was deeply grateful to General Schwartz and Air Force Secretary Michael Donley. As a nonpilot, I was a nontraditional pick, but both gentlemen were willing to give me this opportunity. I assured them I would do my best.

As I departed the Joint Staff I could not help but reflect on the wonderful opportunity I had enjoyed. I was honored to serve two spectacular chairmen of the Joint Chiefs, Adm. Mike Mullen and Gen. Marty Dempsey. Although they differed in personality and leadership styles, both were equally effective. I was humbled to brief and participate in meetings with the secretary of defense and with the service chiefs. I also participated in meetings with the national security advisor, the secretary of state, and the president. My Senate confirmation process to become the thirty-seventh vice chief of staff of the Air Force was completed quickly and without incident. Now it was a matter of a brief promotion ceremony and I would start my journey as a four-star general!

8

#37

A dream doesn't become reality through magic;
it takes sweat, determination and hard work.

—GEN. COLIN POWELL (RET.)[1]

My emotions the morning of Friday, July 27, 2012, ranged from disbelief to extreme humbleness and honor. It was the day I pinned on my fourth star, and my anticipation level was palpable. When I enlisted in 1971, no African American, of any military service, had achieved the rank of four stars. There are no words to describe the feeling of joining this elite club. There was a modest promotion ceremony scheduled for midmorning, and my family members gathered at my home on Bolling AFB to caravan over to the Pentagon. Air Force chief of staff Norty Schwartz officiated the event, and in what would become a classic photo that was printed and reprinted across the Air Force, my two sons pinned on my fourth star as the thirty-seventh vice chief of staff of the Air Force.

The Air Force vice chief of staff is a great leadership opportunity and a critical job for our nation's security. My job was to assist the Air Force chief of staff in leading more than 600,000 active-duty, guard, and reserve airmen across the globe, to include managing billions in sophisticated aircraft, satellites, intercontinental ballistic missiles, two thirds of our nation's nuclear arsenal, and much more. The vice chief attends most of the high-level Pentagon meetings and oftentimes attends the "Tank," which is a meeting between the chairman of the Joint Chiefs of Staff, the service chiefs, and occasionally the secretary of defense or the president. Following the promotion ceremony, General Schwartz asked if I was ready for this challenge, and my response was, "Absolutely!"

My plan was to ease into the job by requesting orientation briefings to better understand the current issues, but that was not to be. On Sunday following the Friday ceremony, I said goodbye to my out-of-town family guests and boarded an airplane to Robins AFB, Georgia, to officiate a retirement and change of command ceremony for the outgoing and incoming commanders of the Air Force Reserve. I returned to Andrews AFB, Maryland, late Monday afternoon, assuming I would head home for the day. As I stepped into the car that was waiting on the flight line, however, my executive officer handed me a book to study and informed me of a meeting in the Tank in thirty minutes. When I arrived home at 9:00 p.m. that night, Ora asked how my first day had been. My response was, "You have no idea!"

First thing Tuesday morning, I pulled into my parking space on the river entrance of the Pentagon. As I exited my vehicle and headed toward the majestic steps leading up to the Pentagon, I was nearly brought to tears. Since August 2006 I had walked up those stairs, barely noticing the official black sedans parked behind me. The vehicles belonged to the Pentagon motor pool and were staged in place each day to transport high-ranking Pentagon officials to various meetings and events around the city. Nearly all the drivers were African American, many of whom had served as enlisted members in the military. I knew only a few of them by name, but I was always careful to greet them as I arrived and departed each day.

On this day, my second as a four-star general, about ten of the men exited their vehicles and met me at the bottom of the stairs. One of the gentlemen, whose face belied years of struggle and hardship, spoke up and said he and his fellow drivers just wanted to express their pride in my promotion. They explained that they had watched me walk up those stairs for six years, initially as a one-star general, and their hearts were filled with pride. But now that I was a four-star, they could no longer sit quietly inside their sedans; rather, they wanted to express just how proud they were to see an African American four-star general, particularly because during their period of service, black officers, much less black general officers, were indeed a rare sight.

It's difficult to express what it's like to become a four-star general in the military. It's particularly hard to convey life as a black four-star. Since its creation in 1947, the Air Force has promoted only nine African American general officers to four stars, so it is an unusually rare occurrence. As much as I was humbled and thankful for my opportunity to serve at this grade, it is akin to celebrity status. From visiting Air Force installations around the globe to speaking at local events to stopping by a local 7-Eleven convenience store, wearing four-star rank engenders immediate respect and admiration by most, an occurrence and experience that I will always cherish.

As I entered my E-Ring office on the fourth floor of the Pentagon, I started to unpack my belongings. During most of my career, I kept a Bible on my desk for inspiration, so I placed it in the right corner. I had also displayed two of my favorite paintings: one was the popular portrait of President George Washington kneeling in prayer next to his horse, and the other was a painting of a Tuskegee airman with his P-51 Mustang aircraft in the background. These were three constants that had followed me through most of my career, and I was careful as I found just the right spots for the portraits.

I was interrupted by my executive officer, who explained a large group of staff members needed to brief me on an important topic. I paused my office décor work for a one-hour meeting where there were barely enough chairs for everyone to be seated. Following the meeting, I returned to my unpacking chores when the executive officer entered again, this time stating the senior Air Force lawyer (referred to as the judge advocate general or TJAG), a lieutenant general who was just in the previous meeting, wanted a word with me. The TJAG entered and said he noticed the George Washington portrait and Bible on my desk and was concerned that they could be viewed by some as offensive.

As a matter of practice, unless specifically asked, I did not discuss my religious beliefs and I neither asked nor was I interested in the religious beliefs of coworkers or subordinates. From my perspective, one's religious beliefs or lack thereof is a personal matter and has nothing to do with work performance. This was not, however, the first time someone had called out my two office treasures, some complimentary and others not. I asked the TJAG if there was any Air Force guidance forbidding their presence. His response was that although both were permissible, his advice was to keep the portrait, since it was such a common portrayal of George Washington, but remove the Bible to ensure no one entering my office would be offended. I declined that advice.

I absolutely loved the vice chief's job. Some say the vice chief does what the chief of staff does not want to do. But my boss, Air Force chief of staff Mark Welsh, never made me feel that way. He gave me leeway to pursue several projects, and he backed me up. Since the chief of staff often travels, the vice chief most often runs Pentagon daily operations and attends most of the meetings. The days and weekends are long and the issues are tough, but the work is thrilling and rewarding. Up to that point in my career, I had enjoyed every job I was given, especially those involving command. But none of my previous assignments matched this opportunity.

Mom's Revelation

As a freshly minted four-star, I was frequently asked to speak at various events. A memorable speaking request came from my Uncle Luther Gaines, a widower still living in my maternal grandparents' home in Cullen, Virginia. Uncle Luther requested I come to Farmville, Virginia, during Black History Month to speak at Moton High School, which had been converted to a museum. I knew Mom had attended Moton High School but had not graduated. With a bit of research, I discovered the significance of Moton High School to the civil rights movement, and Mom's association with the movement.

In 1951, Mom was a junior at Moton. Despite the dictates of the doctrine of separate but equal, Moton's facilities paled in comparison to nearby Farmville High School, attended by whites. Built in 1939 to accommodate 180 students, Moton had no gymnasium, no cafeteria, no science laboratories, and no athletic field. A decade later, when Mom attended, the county had constructed several freestanding buildings, made of plywood and tarpaper, to accommodate a student population that had ballooned to more than 450.

The buildings had no plumbing and were heated by wood stoves. The roofs leaked and the students had to sit with an umbrella open in the classroom when it rained. The amount of money spent by the county on white students at the time was $817 per student compared to $194 for black students. The lack of adequate classroom space actually led to some classes being taught in broken-down school buses. In his memoir *Students on Strike*, John A. Stokes, a fellow student at Moton, described life for "colored" students during that time: "During this time in the South, it was not unusual for colored boys and girls to be taunted, hurt and even killed, especially if they were caught out at night. The white authorities blame us. They ask, 'just why are you all out at this time of night anyhow?' We know we can never get fair treatment from the police. A colored person can't win a case in court. It is our word against theirs. You see all law enforcement officers and elected officials are White."[2]

Conditions at Moton got so bad that the student body decided to protest for better conditions. They accepted that racial segregation was legal but could not accept that the county did not live up to the part of the law that provided the "equal" facilities and services. So, on April 23, 1951, the students, including Mom, walked out of school in protest for better school equipment and conditions. For the remainder of the day, students picketed the school, both inside and outside, with placards proclaiming, "We want a new school or none at all" and "Down with tar-paper shacks."

The remaining history of the Moton High School strike is well documented. The strike led to several lawsuits that culminated in *Brown v. Board of Education of Topeka*, whereby in 1954 the U.S. Supreme Court unanimously decreed that public school segregation was unconstitutional. Unfortunately, this critical part of America's history was not kind to those subsequent black students. Following the strike and the U.S. Supreme Court ruling, Virginia's Prince Edward County officials were so stridently opposed to desegregation that they withheld funding for all county high schools, which meant the students that followed had no high school to attend. To her credit, after raising six children, Mom finally received her high school diploma at age forty-two.

The Stalker

On a restful summer Saturday evening around 6:00 p.m., Ora received a call from a neighbor on the base. "Ora," her friend said, "a few minutes ago I was out for a walk and crossed paths with a disheveled looking woman. She was wearing a hoodie and pushing a baby carriage that was filled with old bags and miscellaneous items but no baby. Just giving you a heads-up because she asked me if I knew where General Spencer lived on the base. Of course I didn't tell her but I thought you should know." Ora mentioned it to me but neither of us thought much about it.

At around 11:00 p.m. that night, I walked to my front door to let out our dog. As I opened the door, I was shocked to see this woman standing on my front porch, baby carriage in tow. When I opened the door to step outside, the dog started barking at the stranger. I did not feel physically threatened but I did not want her inside the house. I greeted her and asked if I could help her. At that very moment, she spotted Ora walking through the house and called out to her. Ora did not know her by name but recognized her face and asked her to come in. I was very uncomfortable with her entering the house, but I figured there would be a brief greeting and she would be on her way.

I anxiously paced the floor as she and Ora began to chat. I discreetly motioned to Ora to cut the conversation short, but the stranger was persistent. Getting a bit more concerned, I searched the house for the emergency duress remote I was issued when we moved into the house just in case I needed it. After a nerve-wracking thirty minutes or so, the woman asked permission to make an overseas call. I refused and told her it was time for her to leave. She then announced that she would like to lie down on our living room floor and spend the night. She also began quoting biblical scriptures and repeating that someone was trying to kill her children.

At that point, it was clear I needed to call the police, but, recognizing that the woman was obviously mentally unstable, I asked her if she would like to speak with a chaplain. When she agreed, I called the number to reach the on-call chaplain, but no one answered. I then stepped outside the house to see if the light was on at the home of the Air Force chaplain who lived just down the street. As I started walking toward the chaplain's house, the phone rang and it was the on-duty chaplain. As I watched the woman speak on the phone with the chaplain, it was evident that he was calming her down. The chaplain convinced her to meet him at the base chapel that was just down the street, and she gathered her baby carriage and departed.

I then called the military police, who said they had been looking for the woman. The next day I was informed that she was the spouse of a military member and had been receiving treatment in a local mental hospital when she suddenly walked out. It's not clear why she specifically singled me out, but I discovered that she had plastered my picture throughout her Facebook page. I was given the option to have her arrested for trespassing, but I declined. Ora and I just wanted her to get the help she needed. Fortunately, I never heard from the woman again.

An Extraordinary Meeting

As the vice chief I had the privilege of often visiting with members of Congress. In 2015, my most memorable and personally impactful congressional meeting was with Congressman John Lewis from Georgia's Fifth District. I am not often awestruck by celebrities, but in this case I was. Walking into his office was like walking into a civil rights museum. His office walls were lined with pictures spanning the civil rights movement. From Martin Luther King Jr. to President John F. Kennedy to President Barack Obama, everyone who was anyone in the struggle for equality had done so with Congressman Lewis. I had several members of my staff with me, and they were equally mesmerized as he described the march across the Edmund Pettis Bridge in Selma, Alabama.

In particular, Lewis recalled that as the six hundred marchers crossed the bridge, a state trooper on horseback ordered the group to disperse. After Lewis' pleas to proceed were rebuffed, he simply asked the officer to allow him a moment to kneel and pray before turning back. As Lewis was about to kneel, the officer and other troopers discharged tear gas and charged into the crowd, running them over with their horses and beating them with nightsticks. In particular, Lewis was struck by one of the officers and suffered a fractured skull.

That was not the only incident where Lewis was physically assaulted. When he was a freedom rider, two white men in Rock Hill, South Carolina, attacked him when he tried to enter a whites-only waiting room. During a CNN interview commemorating the fortieth anniversary of the freedom rides, Lewis spoke about the violence he and twelve other original freedom riders endured. In Anniston, Alabama, He described how, in his bus was firebombed after Ku Klux Klan members deflated its tires, forcing it to a stop. He described how, in Montgomery, Alabama, he was hit in the head with a wooden crate by an angry mob. "It was very violent. I thought I was going to die. I was left lying in the Greyhound bus station in Montgomery unconscious," said Lewis.[3]

I so much admired Congressman Lewis because he took a stand. He took a stand when it was unpopular and some would say life-threatening. He is one of the most courageous people I've known. Beginning at a young age, he recognized the atrocities that plagued the lives of African Americans in our country, and at great personal risk he got off the bench and waded into the fray to make a difference. Today there are so many pundits and critics who lob verbal and Twitter hand grenades into the problems of the day but don't have the courage to get inside the ring. While visiting Congressman Lewis' office, I asked what I perceived to be a profound question: "Where are the John Lewises of today?" I guess I should not have been surprised that it was not my question that was truly profound, but his simple, direct answer: "I'm looking at one right now."

What this civil rights hero was saying is we all have a responsibility to make our country better. Whether by personal example or leading a march, we all have a role to play. America is better when its people speak up and speak out when things are wrong. If we walk past a problem rather than confronting an issue we know is not right, we become part of the problem. Our country was birthed on protest and standing up for freedom. Our history has taught us that freedom is not free. There is a price to be paid for our way of life. Reflecting on that wonderful meeting with Congressman Lewis, a powerful biblical scripture, Luke 12:48, came to mind: "Unto whom much is given, of him much shall be required."

Every Dollar Counts

In July 1963, President John F. Kennedy was enraged while vacationing in Hyannis, Massachusetts. July 25, the president woke to a *Washington Post* article reporting that the Air Force had spent $5,000 at nearby Otis AFB on furniture and other related items (about $40,000 today) for a room for his pregnant first lady to use in the event it was needed. The president was furious over this report, considering it a colossal waste of resources.[4] A critical lesson I learned through my experience dealing with DoD spending is that when it comes to wasting money, not much has changed since 1963. I have seen it firsthand and fought against it at every level in the department. From an overly bureaucratic acquisition process to bloated head-quarters staffs, I am convinced that the DoD could fund many of its recorded shortfalls if they could simply get their arms around the enormous inefficiency.

With my financial background and passion for cost efficiency, the chief of staff allowed me to handle most of the budget and planning issues for the Air Force. In the fall of 2013, as part of a deal to raise the debt ceiling, President Obama and Congress agreed to include a plan to deal with the nation's excessive debt. The Joint Select Committee on Deficit Reduction was formed (also referred to as the "Super Committee," or Simpson-Bowles, from the names of the cochairs Alan Simpson and Erskine Bowles) to recommend legislation that would decrease the deficit by $1.2 trillion over ten years. Included was a sequestration provision that would result in random, across-the-board cuts to government spending that would severely impact DoD funding. Sequestration was intended to be so onerous that no committee of reasonable people would ever fail to reach a bipartisan agreement. Leave it to the U.S. Congress to fail at something that so obviously needed a solution, but that's exactly what happened. They failed.

The sequestration trigger was activated in March 2013 and the result put DoD and other government agencies in a tailspin. In response, we developed a program titled Every Dollar Counts to seek ways to quickly save money and preserve as much Air Force readiness as possible. To comply with the law, we took unprecedented actions to stand down front-line fighter and bomber squadrons just to balance the books. Additionally, the entire DoD was forced to temporarily lay off or "furlough" thousands of civil service employees. Sequestration forced the staff and me to work around the clock seeking ways to quickly, and in many cases inefficiently, curtail spending. From testifying in Congress about the impacts of sequestration cuts to conducting press interviews, tackling the challenges of sequestration was extremely challenging, and much to my chagrin, totally unnecessary and self-inflicted.

The good news was the Every Dollar Counts campaign engendered Air Force–wide support and created bottom-up solutions that significantly improved our efficiency and thus our readiness. The campaign began on May 1, 2013, with a one-month open season on efficiency ideas. I was initially skeptical about how many airmen would participate, but when we received more than 1,700 ideas on the very first day, those notions of skepticism were erased. As we approached the latter part of the month, we had received more than 12,000 ideas. The suggestions came so fast we established a "war room" operation with computers and functional experts to collect the ideas and disseminate them for evaluation.

I was impressed with the quantity and quality of the ideas, and we began to implement them by the hundreds. To my great disappointment, there were many "functional experts" on the Pentagon staff that resented the program and fought against the notion of approving ideas from the field. I remained resolute, however, that the best ideas typically come from the bottom-up and insisted that our default position be to approve the suggestions unless I allowed otherwise. With savings ideas rolling in by the thousands, we naturally focused our attention on larger-dollar-value targets first.

For example, we vigorously pursued the Air Force Community Partnerships initiative, which emphasized the use of both public-public and public-private (P4) partnerships to tap into the intellectual capital and entrepreneurial spirit of installation and community leaders. We did the same with enhanced use leases (EULs) that allowed our installations to identify potential opportunities to leverage unused installation real estate. For example, one of our installations in the Midwest signed an agreement with a local developer to build solar panels on federal land in exchange for the developer building a new gymnasium for the base.

We also implemented the concept of "better buying power," which focused on "should cost" in order to scrutinize each element of cost across the life cycle and assess how cost can be reduced without unacceptable reductions in value received. The cost savings garnered from this initiative were significant. Energy was another area of focus that reaped large cost savings. From increasing tons of cargo moved on a gallon of fuel by flying in a specified formation (similar to formations flown by geese in order to draft off of each other) to installing more efficient engines on the Air Force KC-135 tanker fleet, millions of dollars were saved on the Air Force energy bill alone.

During our campaign, my convictions about DoD inefficiency were only reinforced. For example, it is disappointing to me that each service purchases and uses unmanned aerial vehicles (drones) for intelligence, surveillance, and reconnaissance (ISR) missions when that task can and should be assigned to one service. Several of the military services purchase and operate C-130 aircraft for the tactical airlift mission. This unnecessary duplication results in increased procurement costs and duplicative training, maintenance, and supply chain costs. Unfortunately, competition for resources and the desire to own and control assets is so intense between the services that any meaningful change is unlikely, which is unfortunate. To his great credit, Robert Gates, the twenty-second secretary of defense, took on this inefficiency with a vengeance and with great success. Unfortunately, though, much of what he achieved was disassembled or simply ignored upon his departure.

There are nonprofit associations, the Government Accounting Office, and members of Congress that document and track government waste and inefficiency through published reports every year. Yet little is done to follow up on those reports and make any real progress toward eliminating government waste and excess spending. The 2020 proposed fiscal year budget for the DoD alone was $718 billion, while the estimated U.S. budget deficit exceeds $2 trillion and the U.S. debt exceeds $23 trillion. This is a formula for financial ruin, yet it gets little mention by elected leaders or the media.

A Heinous Crime

President Barack Obama said, "Sexual assault in the ranks is going to make—and has made—the military less effective than it can be. It is dangerous to our national security."[5] Growing up on the Horseshoe, I experienced the intense pressure put on males to have sex. It had little to do with developing a relationship and everything to do with conquest and bragging rights. It was based on a ridiculous notion about manhood. Following a high school football practice, the question was often posed in the locker room, "Is there anyone on the team who has not had sex?" Of course, no one dared admit to being a virgin, although I suspect 90 percent or better were. In hindsight, while this notion seemed silly, it was also the unfortunate reality.

Every day, these negative attitudes toward women graduate from our high schools all over the country and enter our military. Unfortunately, unwanted and inappropriate sexual contact can wrongly be accepted in high school as horseplay and "boys being boys," when in fact it is a crime. Unwanted sexual advances, up to and including rape, are criminal activity that our society and thus our military must resolve. The "Me Too" movement was birthed to combat sexual harassment and sexual assault. It is an acknowledgment that men, particularly powerful men, too often mistreat women, and as a society we must both acknowledge and stop this behavior from happening in the future.

As vice chief of staff, one of my first challenges was to deal with this heinous crime. During my first few weeks in the job, the 2012 Workplace and Gender Relations Survey of Active Duty Members (2012 WGRA) was released, and the results were not good. Overall, the survey showed sexual assault among military members was on the rise and victims were hesitant to report the assaults to military commanders for fear of retribution. The results reverberated across Congress, and the members wanted answers. Some in Congress even proposed taking command-ers out of the process of reporting and prosecuting sexual assault crimes.

At about the same time, a sexual assault bombshell hit the Air Force. A female basic trainee told her military training instructor (MTI) that one of her MTIs had sexually assaulted a female trainee, an allegation that was later substantiated. This report opened a floodgate of follow-on allegations of sexual misconduct and rape that were also subsequently confirmed. In total, forty-nine individuals, three of them men, came forward to say they were victims of rape or sexual assault in basic training. Any sexual misconduct is unacceptable, but that these were perpetrated by MTIs against young trainees was particularly egregious.

Eliminating sexual assault in the Air Force became our top priority, and I was given the task to develop and implement solutions. The Air Force office respon-sible for rooting out this conduct was the Sexual Assault Prevention and Response (SAPR) Office. But their office consisted of only five people buried in the organi-zational structure of our Personnel Directorate. So, as a start, the Secretary of the Air Force approved transferring the SAPR office directly under my supervision, and we quickly increased the office staff to thirty people and we appointed an Air Force major general to head the office. Our new SAPR office conducted dozens of focus groups and engaged SAPR experts from academia, industry, and the Centers for Disease Control.

The more we learned about this complex crime, the more work we had to do. We established a SAPR Council, where we engaged each month with a different Air

Force installation to discuss causes and solutions. We also implemented a pioneering effort to provide special victims counsel for victims of sexual assault. This program was so successful it was implemented across the entire DoD. I also routinely attended SAPR round-table discussions with the secretary of defense and at the White House. I literally worked on this issue every day, and the SAPR office began to break through and make real progress. The number of sexual assaults began to decline while at the same time reporting began to increase. This latter statistic showed that military victims of sexual assault were gaining confidence that their allegations would be taken seriously and, if substantiated, would be dealt with appropriately.

This was a tough issue for me personally. I listened intently to victims of sexual assault as they described the incidents. I could see and feel the hurt and devastation this crime inflicts on its victims. The military cannot be successful without trust, and sexual assault erodes trust and negatively impacts good order and discipline. To be sure, sexual assault is not isolated to the military; it is a societal problem. Most in our society, however, expect more of the military. Parents don't send their children into the military to be sexually assaulted. Unfortunately, sexual predators exist, and some will make their way into the military. During my watch, we treated this crime as a war we were determined to win.

Dignified Transfer

On a crisp fall day I met the Secretary of the Air Force, Debbie James, at the Andrews AFB passenger terminal. We were scheduled to fly to Dover AFB, Delaware, to perform a dignified transfer for a fallen airman. Of everything I experienced in my job as vice chief of staff, none was as solemn and sobering as meeting the remains of an airman killed in action in Iraq or Afghanistan. This was Secretary James' first experience dealing with the death of an airman, so she listened intently during the short flight as I explained the process and the ceremony. The folks who serve at the transfer facility at Dover AFB are among the most professional in the military. They go to great pains to ensure everything is perfect for the fallen and their grieving family members.

When we arrived, the airplane transporting the coffin was about forty-five minutes from landing. So the secretary and I met with family members in a nice facility on the base. As we entered the facility, the gravity of the occasion was immediate. The parents were understandably distraught, and we tried our best to comfort and console them. As I spoke with uncles and aunts of the deceased, their expressions of pride in their loved one's service to our country were heartbreaking. I fought back emotion as they explained that their nephew's only goal in life was to serve in the Air Force and how proud he was to be serving our country.

We stepped quickly as the base officials announced the C-17 cargo aircraft was on final approach. A bus transported us to the flight line, and we aligned ourselves at the position of "attention" as the huge transport airplane taxied toward our position. Family members were not allowed in direct proximity to the airplane so they gathered thirty yards away to witness the ceremony. The ceremony itself is intentionally brief. The coffin is removed from the aircraft and transferred to an awaiting vehicle that will conduct final preparation of the remains.

Our small group consisted of Secretary James, a chaplain, a pallbearer team, and myself. We saluted in unison as the aircraft came to a stop and the pilots shut down the engines. As the on-board crew lowered the rear doors, we marched inside the aircraft and paused for a moment of silence. Then, with great precision, the pallbearers lifted the coffin and moved it to the awaiting vehicle. Finally, we saluted again as the coffin was loaded and the vehicle drove off. As I lowered my salute I heard the sobbing family members viewing the ceremony in the background. They had given their son and nephew in service to our country, and he had made the ultimate sacrifice.

By design and out of respect for the families, dignified transfer ceremonies are private, so most Americans will never actually witness the ceremony unless a family member is involved. During the return flight, however, I could not help but wish that every American could witness what I had just experienced. For too many Americans, war is something that happens overseas and is treated as out-of-sight, out-of-mind. There may be a brief acknowledgment on the nightly news, but it barely captures the attention of most viewers. Americans go about their lives with little thought or acknowledgment that service members are serving in harm's way to protect their freedoms. It's one thing to say young brave Americans are willing to give their lives if necessary to defend our country. It's quite another thing to actually do so.

It's an Honor to Meet You, Mr. President

A distinct advantage of serving as vice chief of staff was the opportunity to represent the Air Force at the White House. As an African American, it was a unique honor to meet and speak with President Barack Obama, the first black president of the United States. My first encounter was during a White House event to commemorate Memorial Day. Each Memorial Day, the White House hosted a breakfast for Gold Star families and the president personally greeted each attendee. As Ora and I progressed toward the front of the long line of attendees, the military aide introduced us to the president. A tall, distinguished-looking gentleman with a slender build, President Obama greeted us with a smile and said, "How are you two this morning? Thank for your service."

I returned the greeting and thanked him for his service to our nation. He also greeted Ora as we posed for a photo and then moved on. During my tenure as vice chief, I had the opportunity to attend meetings and special gatherings with both President Obama and Mrs. Obama. Both are distinguished, polished, and uniquely bright. They broke a glass ceiling that many did not think could be broken. As I watched his hair turn progressively gray, it was apparent that the load he carried as the first African American president was a heavy burden. Yet my encounters with him were always pleasant and respectful.

During my career, I have had the privilege of meeting and interacting with several American presidents. In each case, regardless of political party, I was thoroughly impressed with their demeanor, intellect, and ability to absorb and discern large amounts of critical information. The pressures of the job are enormous and nonstop; there is never a day off, and the divided politics of our time make the most difficult job in the world even more difficult. Yet somehow they possess the uncanny ability to compartmentalize and carryout the nation's business while tuning out the noise.

I've often pondered what our political climate could be if every American had the same opportunity I had to actually meet and interact with their elected president. Despite the heated political rhetoric we often witness and the widening political gap between left and right ideologies, there's something about actually meeting a president that transcends hardened political views. Those encounters tend to highlight that even though we may differ in ideology, presidents are human and fallible, just like the rest of us. Whether Republican, who are attacked by left-leaning media, or Democrat, who are attacked by right-leaning media, the one thing any elected president can count on is a constant barrage of criticism.

Like most Americans, I have my own views on how to solve the tough issues of our time. But, having stood eye-to-eye with Presidents George H. W. Bush, Bill Clinton, George W. Bush, and Barack Obama, with each encounter I walked away with tremendous admiration and respect for them all. Our daily schedules and pressures pale in comparison to the huge weight they shoulder. I was taught long ago that only the toughest problems land on the boss's desk. I am profoundly disappointed how harshly and viciously many attacked these presidents, not just over policy matters, but also on deeply personal issues where even family children were not spared. As Americans, we can and we must do better.

Yes, Even as a Four-Star!

In August 2014, early one weekday morning I was dressed in athletic clothing as I drove into the reserved general officer parking slot at the Joint Base Anacostia-Bolling gym in Washington, D.C. I had an extremely busy day ahead and was rushing to get a quick workout before heading to the Pentagon. I opened my car door to get out, and an anxious gentleman approached me and asked why I was parking in a general officer slot. Before I could answer, he began lecturing me on base policies and regulations. He went as far to say that given their busy schedules, it was important to allow general officers that privilege.

Since this was not my first experience with misplaced stereotypes, rather than get angry, I asked him a simple but pointed question, "Why do you assume I am not a general officer?" At that moment, I could see his facial expression change. He realized that he had a bias that did not accept African Americans as general officers. I then pointed to the four-star emblem on my car windshield, and he sheepishly walked away. To put a finer point on this incident, this individual was African American! Even as a black man, he had fallen victim to the same negative racial profiling as everyone else. Even in 2014 with an African American president of the United States, he could not process someone that looked liked himself as a general officer.

I arrived home late from the Pentagon one night, and it was clear that Ora was agitated. When I asked what was wrong, her voice began to crack. She had attended a senior spouse social at the home of the Air Force chief of staff to get acquainted with her counterparts. Most in attendance were spouses of one- and two-star generals. As she approached a group of several spouses to introduce herself, before she could speak, two of the spouses requested she bring them a drink. Ora responded that she was an attending spouse and not the "help." Rather than apologize, the spouses asked if she knew how they could get a drink.

Neither Ora nor I believed these spouses were bad people with ill intent, but like most Americans, they had been conditioned to make certain assumptions about

African Americans. Being black, Ora didn't fit their definition of a general officer's spouse. As Americans, it is important to recognize that issues of race in our country are real. They are not made up. I am the first to proclaim that America is the greatest country on Earth and I would not want to live anywhere else. I also proclaim that America is not perfect, and until we deal with issues of race, that part of America's history will remain as a roadblock on our journey toward a more perfect union.

I suppose after forty-four years of service I should not be surprised by these occurrences. After all, since the Air Force was created in 1947, there have been only nine African American four-star generals, so why wouldn't it seem abnormal for a person of color to wear that rank? In my case, it was actually rarer for a career financial manager to be a four-star general. Ironically, I never thought of myself as an African American or financial general officer. I considered myself a general officer, period. I did not see myself as a nonrated vice chief of staff; I was the thirty-seventh vice chief of staff of the U.S. Air Force and so proud, grateful, and humbled to be so.

9

CHANGING LANES

If you want to make enemies, try to change something.

—WOODROW WILSON[1]

A s busy as the Pentagon can be, the work pace subsides significantly during the Christmas holiday. It's a time of year when military members take a break and frequently travel out of town to visit family members. Since most of my family was local, I typically covered the office during that period. So during the week of Christmas 2014, I had a lot of free time in my Pentagon office to reflect and think about my future.

The journey from airman basic to four-star general was not easy and was anything but predictable. The most creative scriptwriter could not have conceived a credible plot with such improbable odds. I wandered out into the hallway of my fourth-floor office and took note of the majestic pictures hanging on the walls. These portraits captured every Air Force chief of staff and every Air Force Secretary since the Air Force's birth in 1947. I recalled that when I entered the Air Force, not one African American, woman, or other minority had been promoted to four stars. As my eyes moved from picture to picture, it was painfully obvious that, forty-three years from the day I entered the U.S. Air Force, still not one person of color was displayed among those pictures. At that moment, a young African American Air Force captain passed by and said, "Sir, I'm looking forward to seeing your picture on that wall someday."

I laughed as I greeted the young woman, while only internally acknowledging that her prediction would not become a reality. That's not to say that race is the factor that would deny her prophecy; in fact, there also has never been a nonpilot appointed as Air Force chief of staff and there was no indication that would change in the near future. Nonetheless, the captain's comment distracted my focus long enough to transition my thoughts toward retiring from the Air Force. The year 2015 would mark three years as vice chief of staff and my forty-fourth year in uniform. My drive home that evening was unusually efficient, as many local commuters were not working that week. As I walked into my home on Joint Base Anacostia-Bolling, dubbed the "Vice Chief's house," I announced to Ora that we should plan to retire the summer of 2015.

The vice chief of staff job would be a fitting, yet wholly unforeseeable, way to end my Air Force career. I was always so humbled and honored when total strangers approached me to say how proud they were to see an African American wearing four stars. It was hard for me to comprehend that people actually looked to me for inspiration and motivation. At times it was a heavy burden to bear, but I embraced it as others had before me. I was even more humbled to learn that in recognition of my performance as vice chief of staff, the Air Force approved two named awards in my honor, the General Larry O. Spencer Innovation Award and the General Larry O. Spencer Special Acts and Services Award.

My official retirement date was October 1, 2015, but, accounting for unused leave and transition preparation, my actual departure ceremony was in August. Having served three years as the vice chief of staff was an honor and the best opportunity I could have dreamed of. But the reality was that after forty-four years of service to the U.S. Air Force and twenty-two moves, it was time to close that chapter in our lives. Retiring from the military as a four-star general is not a casual event. There was a retirement party to organize as well as a formal retirement ceremony. Fortunately, I had a great staff that organized all the events, which culminated in a regal and emotional ceremony held inside a large aircraft hangar at Andrews AFB, Maryland.

It's hard to paint an accurate picture of how I felt during the ceremony, but it was akin to an out-of-body experience. I had attended and officiated dozens of retirement ceremonies during my career, but to be on the other side as the actual retiree was surreal. I was a bit anxious leading up to the actual ceremony, but once the Air Force Honor Guard members all stood in place and the Air Force band started to play the national anthem, all the nerves disappeared. With my family members and a host of friends and associates in the audience, it became clear that I was leaving a unique profession. Service in the military is a way of life. Every day, the people you work with and for all have a common bond: we took a solemn oath to support and defend the Constitution of the United States. At its core, we swore to give our lives if necessary to defend our country. There is no higher calling.

Several days after the official ceremony, I received an unexpected honor. About fifteen former senior noncommissioned officers (NCOs), led by retired Chief Master Sergeant Derry Green, hosted a private ceremony in my honor. I had worked with these NCOs over the years and had great respect for them all. In addition to several nice gifts, each NCO made personal comments and reminisced about our time serving together. They respected my achievement as a four-star general but were particularly appreciative of my enlisted time. As I listened to each of them, it was hard to hold back my emotion. They will perhaps never fully appreciate my respect and admiration for their service. Adversaries of the United States fear our military primarily because of our professional enlisted corps. These NCOs epitomized that professionalism and commitment to service and country.

Having worked up to the very last day on active duty, I didn't have much time to think about the next chapter of my life. Shortly before I retired, an assistant to the secretary of homeland security asked about my interest in leading the Transportation Security Administration (TSA). TSA is a big job with responsibilities ranging from airport security to ship and port security. I had known the secretary of homeland security, Jeh Johnson, from his time as the Department of Defense general counsel. He was smart and a superb leader and someone I admired greatly. Whereas it was an honor to be considered for the job, I was concerned about entering an administration that had only one year remaining, so I respectfully declined.

One of my last duties as vice chief of staff was to assist with the preparation of Chief of Staff Mark Welsh's annual speech at the Air Force Association (AFA) technology symposium in Washington, D.C. So it was ironic that concurrently, the twenty-second Secretary of the Air Force, Michael Donley, asked me to consider a job as president of the AFA. The AFA is a nonprofit association with about 90,000 members with the mission of promoting a dominant Air Force. I had been an off-and-on member of the AFA for many years but knew very little about the organization other than the two annual professional development symposiums. But the

AFA was having a tough time with both membership and financial viability, and Donley thought my financial experience could help.

I was initially reluctant to consider this opportunity for three primary reasons: First, at the time of the request for consideration, I was still on active duty with six months remaining until retirement. Since the vacancy was to occur in January 2015, I could not possibly take the job until August of that year. Second, if the AFA were willing to delay filling the position until the summer, I would literally start a new job the day after retirement, against the advice of my mentors, who counseled against accepting any job before taking several months off. Finally, having joined the Air Force shortly after high school graduation, I wanted a break from military life. I have many friends who had a tough time disengaging from the Air Force; I did not. I had tremendous respect for Mr. Donley, though, so I agreed to an interview and was selected for the job, and the AFA agreed to hold the position open until I retired in August 2015.

I was sitting in my Pentagon office when I received the congratulatory call from the AFA chairman of the board. Upon giving me the news, the chairman commented that I didn't sound excited about the opportunity. I assured him that I was looking forward to the challenge and would do everything I could to help the organization get back on solid financial footing, but, truth be told, the pause he detected in my voice was real. It wasn't so much about the AFA, but more about my future. Frankly, I felt I needed more time to figure out what my next professional calling would be, and I was concerned that things were moving too fast. Additionally, at the time, Ora and I had plans to retire in North Carolina, so I made it clear that my tenure would likely not exceed three years or so.

Concurrently, having served as a director while on active duty for the Army, Air Force Exchange Service, and the Air Force Aid Society, I was interested in securing a board position with a publicly traded company. With the help of a good friend, Ms. Sheryl Sandberg, chief operating officer for Facebook, shortly after retirement I joined the board of Whirlpool Corporation, the world's largest appliance company. I was subsequently selected to serve on the boards of the Triumph Group, a company that provides aerospace support to the aircraft industry, and Haynes International, a company that produces specialty metals for high-performance aircraft engines. These board opportunities proved to be extremely enjoyable and significantly expanded my professional growth.

My tenure as president of the AFA almost came to an abrupt halt after just three weeks on the job. A hiring agency working for the National Basketball Association (NBA) contacted me. They were looking for a director of NBA operations and wanted me to consider the job. This was a big job involving significant overseas travel to help expand the NBA abroad. Following a few preliminary conversations, I confessed that even though this was a great opportunity with a salary exponentially higher than that of the AFA, I had given them my word and thus could not accept another position. Besides, I had just signed a two-year lease on a house and was uncomfortable relocating to New York. Despite the protest of my kids, who had visions of free NBA tickets in their heads, I respectfully declined.

Red to Black

Improving the AFA's financial performance was complicated. I met with the capable staff and learned that they were keenly aware of the issues. The AFA had been deficit spending for several years, a trend that could not continue. The core dilemma was that the AFA consisted of a myriad of support programs, all of which were popular and served the AFA's mission. But the AFA's revenue was simply insufficient to support those programs at their current levels. Additionally, there was no consensus on priorities, so determining which programs to reduce or eliminate proved extremely difficult. Some had argued that a nonprofit should provide services, not generate a profit, which we agreed with in principle. But we also agreed that a nonprofit must generate enough revenue to at least be self-sustaining over the long term.

Another interesting dilemma was the AFA governance structure. Unlike any other organization I have been associated with, the AFA actually has two volunteer board positions identified to operationally manage portions of the AFA. More specifically, the AFA has a vice chairman of the board for field operations and a vice chairman of the board for aerospace education. Unlike most board-level positions, which are wholly strategically focused, these two billets actually perform a tactical leadership role. And because they are volunteers, accountability and performance are difficult to assess. Whereas that structure is not necessarily wrong or bad, and the AFA is free to organize itself as it sees fit, it certainly is unusual and provided an additional challenge to navigate.

Of course the opposite side of the financial ledger was revenue, and it was clear that the AFA needed to generate additional funding. So the staff developed a parallel plan to increase revenue. For expense reduction, the staff embarked on a focused effort to list and review every expense line. That review culminated with an intense presentation to the board of directors with recommendations to reduce expenses to programs that were near and dear to many board members. But thanks to the support of the AFA's chairman of the board, former Secretary of the Air Force Whitten Peters, several necessary expenses were curtailed.

Increasing revenue was less controversial but no less difficult. Fortunately, the best targets of opportunity were obvious. The AFA's two signature technology symposiums represented the largest cash-generating opportunities, and they were ripe for expansion and growth. Recognizing the need to have a single person in charge of the expansion, Brig. Gen. Bernie Skoch (Ret.) stepped forward to take on this difficult task, and he performed brilliantly. Skoch was already serving as commissioner of the AFA's successful youth STEM program called Cyber Patriot, which conducted the largest youth cyber defense competition in the country. Despite the additional workload, Skoch, an exceptional leader, agreed to take on this additional task while continuing to lead Cyber Patriot.

Skoch quickly and systematically organized the entire staff around growing both events. Several high performers on the staff, like Meghan McClelland, Barbara Taylor, and others, joined Skoch to achieve exponential growth in attendance and revenue. This widespread success caught the attention of major industry leaders, who flocked to the technology symposiums with both technology exhibits and sponsorship support. The rapid growth also attracted big-name speakers, including Jeff Bezos, Mark Cuban, and then Vice President Mike Pence. A large factor in our success was the strong support from Air Force leadership, who encouraged airmen to take advantage of this unique professional development event. The combination of reduced expenses and increased revenue resulted in a break-even posture the first year, followed by significant surpluses the following two years. This represented an astonishing financial turnaround that put the AFA on strong fiscal footing for the first time in a decade.

Nearly as dramatic was a turnaround in membership growth. By 2015, the AFA's membership had precipitously declined for thirty consecutive years. Working with the staff and a membership committee of dedicated volunteers, we halted the decline in 2016 and began to climb in 2017 and 2018. In fact, total membership was around 93,000 and dropping in 2015, but by the end of 2018 the AFA was close to reaching 100,000 members. Like many membership organizations, gaining new and sustainable members is a tough task, especially among millennials. But with the strong support of our volunteer and paid staff, we managed to turn a tide that had resisted for three decades.

With that success, when I announced my departure effective March 1, 2019, many asked why I was leaving, even though my contract period had expired. The AFA was indeed on a roll, and the path for continued growth and success was clear. In short, why leave a good thing? In fact, things were going well and staff morale was high. I accepted the AFA job primarily because of the financial and membership challenges. I believed that as a team, we could move the AFA out of the red and into the black financially while simultaneously arresting the decades-long decline in membership. Both of these goals were accomplished. There was, however, still considerable runway ahead of us to continue the growth and expansion of the AFA to better serve the Air Force.

As much as I enjoyed working with the staff, many of whom became close personal friends, I began to give serious thought as to how I wanted to spend the remainder of my full-time professional life. The AFA is a great organization and performs a critical mission for the Air Force. In many ways it is a direct arm of the Air Force, which, oddly enough, is something that bothered me. I loved every day of my forty-four-year Air Force career, and I still bleed Air Force blue. But after forty-four years in uniform and more than three years at the AFA, I wanted a break. I have many Air Force friends who, although now retired, remain very much engaged in Air Force issues, and for them the AFA serves as a vehicle to extend their active duty. But, while some consider that admirable, that is not who I am. I wanted something different to expand into other interests and move on from the Air Force.

I have many curiosities and passions. I love the business world and am as passionate about serving on the board of the Whirlpool Corporation as I was about serving the world's best Air Force. I enjoy and feel an obligation to support local community events through my church. I have personal family goals, and I like getting my hands and elbows greasy working on my 1972 Chevrolet Monte Carlo. I've even been encouraged to dabble in politics, but I have resisted thus far. My strongest calling is to lead. The thought of leading and growing a business is intriguing and is something I would jump at if offered the opportunity.

While serving at the AFA, I admired the volunteers who unselfishly gave their time and talent toward a great organization. I also loved interacting with airmen in every grade to provide the best professional development opportunity anywhere. Throughout my tenure we worked hard to expand the AFA's membership tent, especially among our enlisted force. We also worked assiduously to achieve greater diversity among the AFA's leadership and board structure, with some success but not nearly enough. I departed the AFA proud of what the team had accomplished. I had a great staff and a great boss, and for that I am truly grateful. A former chief of staff of the Air Force wrote me a personal note stating, "We had accomplished more for AFA since Jimmie Doolittle in 1946." That message humbled me, but, as I responded back to him, I certainly can't compare myself to General Doolittle, and any credit belongs to the hard work and dedicated support of the thousands of AFA volunteers and the dedicated and committed staff.

As I had done three and a half years before, I worked until my last day at the AFA and did not secure another full-time job prior to departure, but this time it was by design. My goal was to take the summer of 2019 off to work down a long honey-do list and think about my future. During that period I spent hours in the Fort Belvoir gymnasium and assisting Ora with her flower garden. I also spent time reading, praying, reflecting, and taking long walks with my dog. The conclusion of my reflection was twofold: First, I was not ready for retirement. I still enjoy full-time employment, and, following a restful summer, I was ready to go back to work. Second, I wanted to find another leadership opportunity, but ideally for an organization that supports America's public servants. At the time, I had no particular organization in mind, but those factors were on my wish list.

To my great fortune, in the fall of 2019 one of my great mentors, Gen. Hal Hornburg, USAF (Ret.), notified me of an opportunity that was just what I was seeking. He presented an opportunity to compete for president of the Armed Forces Benefit Association (AFBA). The AFBA is a wonderful organization that provides membership benefits, such as low-cost term life insurance, to military members, first responders, federal civilian employees, and contractors and their families. The AFBA has a rich history that began with Gen. Dwight D. Eisenhower, who helped establish the AFBA in 1947. The original office was in the basement of the Pentagon. At the time, life insurance that would pay a death benefit if the member was killed in combat was not available. The AFBA was established to fill that void and continues to do so today.

In January 2020, I was humbled and honored to receive notification of my selection as their new president. Ironically, in mid-March 2020, after only two days in the job, the state of Virginia declared a work-from-home policy in response to the COVID-19 pandemic. That is certainly not the beginning I envisioned, but in hindsight the crisis quickly highlighted the exceptional talent that was inherent in the staff. Also, in June 2020, I was named dual president of the AFBA and of our underwriter for-profit company, 5Star Life Insurance Company, which is another great organization with a strong staff. This was an answer to prayer as it offered the unique opportunity to lead for-profit and nonprofit companies simultaneously. As much as I enjoyed the Air Force and the AFA, I truly love my job at the AFBA/5Star Life and hope to serve for a long time.

10

LIFE LESSONS

Life is a succession of lessons which
must be lived to be understood.

—RALPH WALDO EMERSON[1]

"In my life I have lived, I have loved, I have lost, I have missed, I have hurt, I have trusted, I have made mistakes, but most of all, I have learned."[2] A benefit of living such a fulfilling and diverse professional career is the opportunity to share those experiences with various groups around the country. When doing so, I am frequently asked to talk about life lessons I might pass on to others starting out in their careers. I don't for a minute believe I possess the secrets to professional success. But as a believer in the biblical principle that "from those to whom much is given, much is required," I am happy to summarize and provide my thoughts based on my journey as a once dark horse.

Life Lesson One: Even a Dark Horse Can Succeed

When Dad was admitted for surgery at Walter Reed in January 2009, we couldn't imagine at the time that he would never return home. I chuckled a bit when visiting him while in uniform because as an old enlisted man, he made a point to let the medical staff know I was a two-star general, the implication being they had better take good care of him. Before one particular visit, I had recently been informed about my nomination for a third star. I was told not to discuss the news until the

White House had approved the official nomination announcement. As I sat next to his bed, I agonized over whether to let him in on the news. I badly wanted to because I knew he would be so proud and it might raise his spirits, but I figured formal approval would come soon enough, so I kept the secret to myself. It is something I regret to this day.

It's hard to say why on this day he confided in me in a way he never had before, but, sitting up in his bed, he began to talk about how tough his experience had been as a young soldier in the U.S. Army during the 1940s, '50s, and '60s. I guess it had never occurred to me that he entered the military before it was desegregated. And even after legal integration, black soldiers continued to be treated poorly. Listening to him talk about segregated and substandard facilities and being relegated to menial tasks broke my heart. He had to overcome so many obstacles during his life; my challenges paled in comparison.

Yet he endured and built a successful life for our family. The odds of success were stacked against him, but he persevered anyway. He was assigned to Army installations where some facilities were off-limits because of his race. He lived in communities that displayed signs proclaiming "no coloreds allowed." For reasons I cannot comprehend, he was never bitter or spiteful. As his father before him, he picked up the cards life had dealt him and played them to the best of his ability. A clear lesson I learned from him that day was that "it's not how you start the race that counts most, but how you finish the race." At the time, I didn't realize his race would soon end, but I did know that if I was willing to work and sacrifice for it, I could achieve any ambition.

During the 1993–94 school year, I was privileged to attend the Industrial College of the Armed Forces (ICAF) at Fort McNair, Washington, D.C. ICAF is a prestigious military graduate-level training school that only a select few get to attend. During that year, as a class project I volunteered to tutor a young girl from a local southeast D.C. elementary school. Her name was Jennifer—a wonderful young girl and smart as a whip. The tutoring sessions were twice each week, and her face lit up when she saw me enter the school. We generally covered basic math, science, and English, but mostly she wanted to talk about her life.

Like me, she was being raised in the inner city. She was the youngest of several siblings in a single-parent household. Her mother worked at a low-wage job, and it was obvious they were in a tight financial situation. They resided in subsidized and substandard housing. On a few occasions I was tempted to offer her money, but the rules of the tutor program prohibited it. She described fights and hearing gunshots at night. She had two dreams for her life: one was to be a ballerina and the other a veterinarian, which she called an animal doctor. At that young age, she commented to me that she understood that achieving her goals would be an uphill climb, but she was willing to do whatever it took to get there.

My Dad's and Jennifer's situations reinforced what I inherently knew and lived, which was that a dark horse can indeed succeed, but it takes a lot of hard work, perseverance, and commitment. Unfortunately, I know people from all walks of life who were born into less-than-ideal situations but don't want to put in the work. Rather, they blame the "system," and they blame others for their status in life. Trust me, I know the professional playing field is not level, and every American should recognize that fact and work to correct the imbalance. But in my view, the best way to make things better is to work your way into a position of authority so you can assure fairness within your sphere of influence. My gruff grandfather once told me, "Life is not fair; get over it." Coleman Cox said, "I am a great believer in luck. The harder I work, the more of it I seem to have."[3] I think both quotes are sound advice.

Life Lesson Two: Be an Ant, Not a Grasshopper

Two of the most impactful traits I learned growing up were hard work and frugality. "The Ant and the Grasshopper," one of Aesop's fables, taught us about the wisdom of both. While serving in the military, I had many senior leaders tell me their job was to prepare for war, not manage resources or fret over money. I fundamentally reject that notion. Being a warfighter and a good steward of taxpayer dollars are not incompatible concepts. Both can and should be part of any leader's portfolio. While serving in the military, I treated government money as though it was my own because, as a taxpayer, it was my money. I challenged every purchase and scrutinized every requirement, and in doing so I was rewarded and recognized throughout my career.

When I graduated from basic military training in 1971, my monthly salary was $134.40, so I know what it's like to live paycheck to paycheck. In fact, in those days of paying for goods and services by check and cash, I used the "float" (time it took for a written check to clear the bank) to compress the time between paydays. We shopped for used items in the thrift shop. We carefully timed commissary visits a day or two before payday. I serviced my own vehicle. We raised a large garden and worked part-time jobs. At home I served as barber, painter, plumber, and grounds-keeper. Recreation consisted of visits to free local parks. We found that in many cases, it's not so much how much money we made, but rather how we managed the money we did make.

In 1999 I was the Air Base wing commander at Hill AFB, Utah. This was when Salt Lake City, Utah, began gearing up to host the 2002 Winter Olympics, so there was construction activity throughout the area. Over the years, nearby Hill AFB had demolished many old buildings' concrete bases. With no reasonable disposal options, the broken concrete pieces had been stacked on the backside of the base. I referred to this eyesore as Concrete Mountain. After doing a little research, we discovered a machine that could crush the large concrete chunks into a fine derivative that could be repurposed to construct new roads and highways. Armed with that knowledge, we invited a local construction supervisor to visit Concrete Mountain. We were hoping for an opportunity and perhaps a deal that the contractor would haul away the mountain free of charge. We were pleasantly surprised, though, when the contract supervisor began making offers to purchase the used concrete.

While serving as vice commander of the Oklahoma City Air Logistics Center, the overhaul time for a KC-135 tanker aircraft had been 300 days. But it was unacceptable to commanders to have their airplanes spending nearly a year in our depot. By applying Lean/6-Sigma efficiency tools, the repair time was reduced to an average of 180 days.

During a contract review at Seymour Johnson AFB we found our grounds maintenance contract paid to cut grass in fields where no grass existed. Similarly, we were paying for trash cans to be emptied in buildings that had long been demolished.

Although my industry experience tells me they operate much differently from the military, the challenges are similar. In industry, one would be hard-pressed to find senior managers with a "mission over cost" attitude. Any successful business scrutinizes expenses, revenue, and competitive pricing. The bottom line in business is profit, so there is no room for excessive or extravagant spending. Unlike the military commanders I worked with, industry leaders are specifically evaluated on their ability to cut costs and maximize profit. Yet over time, even in industry, costs and inefficiency can and do creep in when business is going well, and it's typically during the down times when businesses bear down and recommit to cost efficiencies.

Throughout my professional career, the environment for saving resources was target-rich, both in and out of the military. Whenever we made cost savings a priority, we repeatedly found inefficiencies and waste. To be fair, I don't believe we should defend our nation on the cheap, and I do not subscribe to being penny-wise and pound-foolish. If we must go to war, I want our troops to have the best training and the best equipment. I don't believe in winning a war by a score of 51–49. If conflict is necessary, America should completely dominate any opponent foolish enough to engage. Taking an efficient and frugal approach to managing resources, however, frees up money for additional mission readiness. As was the case of the grasshopper, there is nothing wrong with taking a little leisure time. But for long-term efficiency and financial stability, I prefer to be an ant.

Life Lesson Three: Leadership Matters

Famed college basketball coach John Wooden said, "The leader must set the example, not only in areas of right and wrong—character, of course—but elsewhere."[4] Whether leaders are born or made is a topic for great debate. Martin Luther King Jr. was certainly born gifted with great oratorical skills and was a leader of the civil rights movement. Michael Jordan was clearly blessed with impeccable athletic skill and a strong will to win that led the Chicago Bulls basketball team to unprecedented success. Albert Einstein was born with intellectual capacities for physics and mathematics that few have been able to replicate. Likewise, William Shakespeare's mastery of the English language and poetry are considered by many to be genius.

Yet we have all witnessed otherwise ordinary people become extraordinary leaders. In my view, whether leaders are born or made makes for fascinating debate, but it is indisputable that being a strong leader is critical to a successful professional life. As a squadron commander I faced perhaps the ultimate test of leadership during Operation Desert Shield/Storm. In early August of 1990 I attended what I anticipated to be a typical weekly staff meeting with the wing commander, but on this day the topic was anything but typical. My peers and I were given a briefing on the status of Saddam Hussein's advances into Kuwait, and it was apparent the United States was drawing a line in the sand. It was also evident that the 4th Fighter Wing at Seymour Johnson AFB, North Carolina, would play a key role.

Rather than rush back to my squadron and brief everyone, I took a short detour to the base park to gather my thoughts. The airmen in my squadron were mostly junior in rank, so few of them had deployment experience. As I drove away from the park I felt inspired. Not at the prospect of going to war but by the opportunity to lead the unit when it mattered most. Seymour Johnson AFB was being asked to stand up against a brutal regime, and although our squadron mission was to provide financial support for the war, we would do so to the absolute best of our ability. As I walked into my office I asked my assistant to call a mandatory emergency meeting. Twenty minutes later, I walked into the packed room and my first sergeant called everyone to attention.

I immediately put everyone at ease and looked around the room. They had heard the talk of war on the news, and I could see the anxiety in their eyes. I calmly explained the tactical situation and then went into detail about how critical our support was to the war effort. Soon, hundreds of base airmen would prepare to deploy. That meant we had to ensure their finances were in order, and we had to deploy several of our folks forward to work the financial requirements at the deployed location. From the start of my command, I had told the squadron our job was to fly, fight, and win. I reminded them that our wing could not fight effectively if airmen were worried about their pay or commanders could not purchase the necessary supplies and equipment. At the end of my presentation I said, "Folks, this is what we have trained for—its go time."

I'm not sure what reaction I expected, but I was not prepared for what happened next. The entire group, civilians included, jumped to their feet, yelling and hooting and chanting "fly, fight, and win." What followed was a magnificent performance in wartime financial support. Our folks worked around the clock to ensure that every detail was accounted for and every airman was ready to board the departing airplanes. As aircraft arrived to transport troops overseas, I boarded the second airplane to depart, which we called "chalk number two," to wish our initial cadre of three finance troops well. They were sitting on web seats along the outer perimeter of the C-141 transport aircraft with their feet resting against a pallet of equipment occupying the midsection of the aircraft. The senior member of the group, a master sergeant, had a briefcase full of checks and cash that he was holding onto for dear life.

We quickly covered instructions to secure the money when they landed, and I asked that they contact me as soon as possible upon arrival. The junior person on the initial team was a senior airman (E-4) and was clearly a bit shaken. He looked at me and said, "Major, are you coming with us? I'd feel a whole lot better if you were." I responded, "Airman, I have already volunteered to deploy, so if approved,

I'll be right behind you." At that point, the aircraft loadmaster announced that it was time to depart, so I had to leave the aircraft. As I turned to climb down the aircraft steps, the master sergeant whispered to me, "Sir, I hope you can join us soon."

Over my professional career, leadership has always mattered because it's about people. I have learned that most people will follow if they believe the leader genuinely cares about them and has their best interest at heart. My troops wanted me to lead by example, back them up when they were right, and take swift disciplinary action when warranted. Leadership techniques I found particularly effective were: display absolute integrity; develop a clear vision for the organization; communicate clearly, effectively, and often; lead by walking around; allow subordinates to fail and learn; create an environment of innovation and recognize those that excel. Those tools and concepts are not new but for me they proved to be powerful, in peace and during war.

Life Lesson Four: Issues of Race Remain Persistent in American Society

If there was any doubt that deep fissures of race remain persistent in our society, one need only look at the events of spring 2020 for confirmation. During that spring our nation exploded into protests following the tragic death of George Floyd at the hands of local police officers, which had been preceded by a string of disturbing incidents, including the killing of Ahmaud Arbery, who was chased down in broad daylight near Atlanta, Georgia, and shot on the street by men who were purportedly concerned citizens. Tragically, that incident was followed by yet another shooting, of Jacob Blake in Kenosha, Wisconsin, who appeared to be unarmed. These and other racially charged episodes lit a fuse that for years had been on a racial injustice powder keg.

People of color have little choice but to deal with issues of race. It is a reality we cannot escape. We give our children the "talk" about how to deal with police. We struggle when encouraging our kids and grandkids to reach for the stars, knowing that the professional playing field is imbalanced. African Americans are pulled over by law enforcement for simply driving while black. We are tracked in department stores like an enemy aircraft on a radar screen. We are frequently the only people of color in professional conference rooms and at office social functions. Even when we make it to the corporate executive room, our ideas are frequently discounted unless it happens to be a "black" issue. I have often been asked two questions related to race: (1) Did I experience personal racism or bigotry in the Air Force, and (2) What is it like to be black in America?

As to question 1, I did not experience personal racism that negatively impacted my military career. To the contrary, all of my supervisors and commanders were nothing less than professional and personally supportive. Incidents described earlier where I was not acknowledged as a senior officer because of my race, however, happened all too frequently. Similarly, my description of my wife being mistaken for an employee during social functions was not an isolated occurrence. When I was a squadron commander I received an inordinate number of inquiries about a young black female captain I supervised who wore her hair in braids, even though the style was permissible. In short, did racism stand in the path of my career progression? Absolutely not. Did I endure racists' acts and comments throughout my career? Absolutely!

As to question 2, like most U.S. citizens, I am a proud American who loves this country. But living in America as an African American is, in a word, exhausting. Like most Americans, I don't wake up every day thinking about my race. But as a person of color, I am constantly reminded that I am a minority, or worse. Our society is programmed to label people by race. Our government collects analytical data segregated by race. Political candidates strategize and invest significant resources to court votes based on race. President Obama was not simply the forty-fourth president of the United States, but he bears a permanent asterisk by his name identifying his race. I am extremely proud of my heritage and the courageous and storied history of African Americans, but the constant focus on race takes a toll over time, so much so that some medical professionals believe it contributes to poor health outcomes.

As an African American, when I enter a department store, stereotypical assumptions are made. Store managers follow and track my actions throughout the store. They have no idea about my character or financial means. They see only one thing—a black man—that stereotypes and unconscious bias have conditioned them to consider suspicious. When I enter an elevator with a woman, she clutches her purse and moves to the far corner of the small square space. I have been pulled over in my vehicle more times than I can remember, but I have never been cited for any violation. It's hard to find words to describe the pain I have felt when confronted with mistreatment and racism. But, over time, I have been conditioned to suffer in silence.

The questions of racial inequality are even more perplexing when the ongoing and persistent disparities between whites and blacks are considered. The wealth gap between a typical middle-class black household and a similar white household is actually worse today than it was when the Civil Rights Act of 1968 was passed.[5] My parents and grandparents preached that education was the key to success and prosperity, with which I generally agree. But "the typical black household headed by someone with an advanced degree has less wealth than a white household with a high school diploma. Also, only 44% of black households own their homes compared to nearly 74% of whites. In fact, the black homeownership rate has changed little from the late 1960s, while whites have made steady gains over time."[6]

These socioeconomic disparities go beyond the size of one's bank account and owned property. COVID-19 has been especially hard on the black community. Because African Americans are overrepresented in service industry jobs, the combination of not being able to work from home coupled with close and frequent interaction with the public contributed to the unbalanced tally of infections and deaths. Also, during the pandemic, "more than 1 in 5 black families reported they often or sometimes do not have enough food—more than three times the rate for white families."[7] Fewer blacks have robust health insurance, which has led to untreated health conditions, such as high blood pressure and diabetes, rendering them more vulnerable to the virus.

I don't have the answers to America's lingering dilemma regarding race. I do know that children are not born as racists or bigots. At some point in their lives, adults teach that behavior to them. I also know that the only way to solve this challenge is for Americans of good will to stand up and, as the late Congressman John Lewis did, "Get in good trouble, necessary trouble."[8] A quote attributed to Albert Einstein states, "The world is a dangerous place, not because of those who are evil, but because of those who look on and do nothing."[9] Issues of race don't have to define us as Americans. I look forward to a time when race is not such a dominant force in our lives. When will that time come? The choice is ours to make.

Life Lesson Five: Prioritize Career and Family Choices

There are few absolutes in life, but one thing is certain: at some point, everyone has to either leave or retire from their job. When that inevitability occurs, a key consideration will be: Is your family still intact? Life for military families is hard. During my Air Force career, we endured twenty-two moves. Frequent deployments and permanent relocations can take a toll on a marriage and on children. Frequent moves can take on an air of adventure when kids are young, but as they get older or when a spouse finds a career that is fulfilling and financially advantageous, unplanned and untimely moves can become quite disruptive to a family.

Climbing the corporate ladder and chasing that next promotion can also put a strain on families. Working late and volunteering for the tough projects may get you noticed by the top brass, but at what cost? I was fortunate in my career to be promoted ahead of my peers. In doing so, however, I endured a demanding job in the Pentagon as a first lieutenant, worked two jobs as a captain, led a squadron through Operation Desert Storm as a major, and much more. Every one of those assignments was challenging, thrilling, and career-enhancing. But every one of those assignments robbed me of valuable family time that I can never recover, something I would change if I could.

A question I am frequently asked in this regard is, "Can I do both?" That is, can I become a company CEO or serve in a top White House position or serve in the top enlisted grade in the military, and still devote the time required to keep my family unit strong? My answer to that question is yes, but it takes a lot of hard work, planning, and open communication to do it. Over the years, I have had the privilege of speaking with several CEOs of major companies. During each encounter, I asked how, with such demanding work schedules, they managed work-life balance.

With some minor variations, their responses were similar, and each emphasized two major points: communication and choice. No one can successfully lead a large organization without the support of his or her family, and open and honest communication with family members is critical. When I was assigned to the White House, I could not help but notice that the work schedule of the national security advisor (NSA) was brutal. Not only were the hours long, but the issues were hard. Twenty-four/seven, day in and day out, the NSA was point person for every hot-button issue that occurred around the globe.

As vice chief of staff, I had the opportunity to occasionally attend meetings with the NSA. During one of those meetings, the subject of work-life balance was discussed. The NSA was candid about the long hours and regrets over missing valuable family time. He explained, however, that before accepting the job, he and his family had a long conversation about the rigors of the job, and he asked for their input before deciding. During that family discussion, he was honest about the likelihood of missing his children's activities and maybe even vacations. But in his case, his family understood the gravity of the job and its importance to the nation's security and wholeheartedly supported him.

Conversely, I have a friend who is extremely talented and a great leader. She was offered a prestigious job at a law firm that would put her on a path to stardom. But she is a free spirit at heart, and she very much valued her vacation time, where she loved to hike in remote mountain areas. The thought of working around the clock with little time off and being tied to an email account and a cell phone is not what she valued in life. She was clear-eyed about the opportunity she was turning down, but the joy of hiking a trail through the woods on a nice day outweighed any promise of fame and financial security. The good news is that when it comes to deciding on work-life balance, there is no wrong answer. It is an individual decision that is situationally dependent.

I view work-life balance as work-life choice. If offered the opportunity to accept a career-enhancing yet personally demanding job, decide, with the help of your family, if the sacrifice is worth the reward. If yes, go for it. If not, then don't accept the job. Family is clearly more important than any career opportunity. My only caution is you then must live with your decision. Quite often I have seen people, for very good reasons, decide to forgo a challenging job opportunity, and I have then watched those same individuals complain about not getting that big promotion or increase in salary. Again, life is about choices. Understand what is at stake, make a choice, and live with the consequences. At the end of the day, whether serving in the military, industry, nonprofit, or as a volunteer, working can be important business, but working is also family business.

Life Lesson Six: "It's Okay to Try and Fail, But It's Not Okay Not to Try"

Those words spoken to me by my grandfather while plowing a field on his isolated farm guided my life from that point forward. There were times I wanted to give up, but those words rang in my ear as inspiration to never stop trying. Time and time again, I was knocked down but was undeterred. I failed my first calculus test, which jeopardized my earning a bachelor of science degree, but I bore down the following semester and earned a B+. As a captain, my first briefing to our two-star boss was a disaster, but I asked for another chance. Not only did the second try go much better, but the boss rewarded me with additional opportunities.

Gen. Lloyd "Fig" Newton (Ret.) is one of nine African American airmen to achieve four-star rank. As a young officer, Newton was an accomplished fighter pilot who flew 269 combat missions during the Vietnam War. From the onset of his Air Force career, Newton had a burning desire to become a member of the Air Force's elite flying demonstration team, the Thunderbirds. Newton applied two times and was summarily rejected each time until finally he was selected on his third try. In 1974, he became the first African American Thunderbird pilot, holding three positions on the team during his four-year tenure. Newton went on to become a command pilot with more than four thousand flying hours and was promoted to four-star general in 1997.

With the benefit of hindsight, General Newton reflected on that experience with some interesting observations: "From the time I was commissioned a second lieutenant, my goal was to become a Thunderbird pilot. Once I started flying, I realized I was as good as any other fighter pilot, and that gave me the extra drive to pursue my goal. Even though I was turned down twice, I never wavered and I never lost confidence. In fact, those tryouts provided valuable exposure to the Thunderbirds operation that helped me eventually get selected." General Newton's advice to others is, "Don't ever stop trying. I had peers tell me I was wasting my time because the Air Force will not select an African American for the Thunderbirds. My response was I'm not applying to be the first African American Thunderbird pilot. Rather, I want to join the Thunderbird team because that is my dream."[10]

Michael Jordan, arguably the greatest basketball player ever, was released from his high school team, but he didn't give up. Bill Gates's first business venture was a miserable failure, but he became one of the richest people in the world. Benjamin Franklin dropped out of school at age ten, but he invented the lightning rod and bifocals and became one of our nation's founding fathers. Stephen King's first novel was rejected thirty times, yet today his books have sold more than 350 million copies. Thomas Edison failed a thousand times before creating the light bulb. There are many examples that demonstrate what we might accomplish if we don't give in to failures. Failure is inevitable and success is not guaranteed. But if we don't try, we certainly will not succeed.

Life Lesson Seven: Be Kind

A disheveled gentleman stood in front of me in a popular fast-food restaurant. He stepped up to the counter and made his food order. The busy cashier said, "That will be $4.35, please." The gentlemen took out his wallet and showed the empty billfold to the cashier. He explained that he was out of work and had no money. He went on to say he had not eaten all day and requested forgiveness for the bill. The cashier appeared sympathetic but explained she had no authority to provide food free of charge and began to cancel his order. I interrupted the cashier and requested she put his order on my bill. The cashier complied with my request and handed the food to the gentleman, who thanked me and went on his way.

In this tough and oftentimes unfriendly world we live in, I believe we should offer acts of kindness as often as we can. Over the years, I have owned five different 1972 Chevrolet Monte Carlo vehicles. My first purchase was in 1975. For reasons I cannot explain, several years later I made the unwise decision to trade that car in for a much smaller used compact car. That car was too small for our family and started to fail a few months after purchase. While driving the car home from work one day, the fan blade literally fell off the engine and the car came to an abrupt stop. There were no cell phones in those days, so I picked up the fan off the highway and stood by the car with no idea what to do next.

Seemingly out of nowhere, a gentleman pulled his car up behind me, got out, and asked to look under my hood. As it turned out, my water pump was shot and apparently had not been properly installed. There was an auto parts store nearby, so the gentleman drove over to the store, purchased a new water pump, and returned. He then retrieved his tool box from his trunk, spread a blanket under the front of my car, changed my water pump, and reinstalled my fan blade, all on the side of the highway. When he completed his work, he suggested I consider purchasing another make and model car, and then he went on his way. I thanked him profusely and only remembered later that I neither knew his name nor paid him for the new water pump. This act of kindness and compassion is something I will never forget.

I was a runner for more than forty years and during that time I ran nearly every day. Because of the daily pounding, I have endured just about every sports injury that exists. I've had surgery on my knee, and a doctor once told me I have the worst case of heel spurs he had ever seen. Probably the injury that slowed me the most is my hips. Over the years, the accumulated mileage has taken such a toll on my hip joints that I will likely need hip replacement surgery at some point. One day, while out walking our dog, I somehow got tangled up in some wire and took quite a tumble onto the sidewalk. I managed to hold onto the dog leash, but because of my hip discomfort, with nothing to hold on to, I was having a tough time getting back on my feet.

I did not have my cell phone and was getting quite concerned while literally on my knees on a sidewalk adjacent to a busy highway. Exasperated, I decided to sit down for a few minutes and think through a solution. While sitting there, I noticed a vehicle that had sped by turning around at the top of the hill. The woman, who turned out to be a runner herself, pulled her car to the side of the road and gave me a hand up. Once on my feet I was fine, but she then offered to take the dog and me home or to the hospital if I was in pain. I declined the assistance and thanked her for stopping to help a complete stranger. Her response was, "There is no such thing as a stranger when someone is in need."

When Dad was transported from Japan to Walter Reed to recover from the loss of his left hand in the Korean War, he met what turned out to be a lifelong friend, Mr. George Crocker. Sergeant Crocker had also been wounded during the Korean War with gunshots to his abdomen. In an act of mutual kindness, for meals Dad pushed Sergeant Crocker to the dining area in his wheelchair, and in return Sergeant Crocker assisted Dad with handling his utensils and cutting his meat.

In 1974 I endured the long return flight from Taiwan to Los Angeles. I was a senior airman (E-3) and dressed in my uniform. While sitting in LAX waiting for my flight to Washington, D.C., a gentleman noticed me rubbing my knees and asked if I was in pain. I commented about my long overseas return flight and how my long legs had caused my knees to get a bit cramped. He joked about how airplanes are not built for tall people and turned back to the book he was reading. I then made a visit to the restroom in preparation for boarding. When I returned, the attendant announced that first-class passengers should board first, so I sat quietly waiting for my section to be called.

As I sat there, an attendant walked over and reminded me that I could board as a first-class passenger. I laughed and said, "I wish I could afford to sit in first class." She then informed me that the gentleman I had spoken with paid to have my ticket upgraded and wished me a "pain free" flight to D.C. Having never flown in first class, I was thrilled to have the extra legroom, not to mention the VIP service. As I took my seat I noticed the same gentleman sitting across from me, so I leaned over and thanked him. He was a businessman and frequent flyer and said he sympathized with the lack of legroom in the coach section. He went on to say that for years his goal has been to do something kind for at least one person every day of his life. He said the best way to thank him would be for me to help someone else when the opportunity presented itself.

As I watch our country and indeed our world become less civil, I worry sometimes that people mistake kindness for weakness. There is absolutely nothing weak, unmanly, or unwomanly about being kind. While playing football, some of the nicest guys I knew would take your head off on the field. Today, as we face a global pandemic, the acts of kindness displayed by many of our health care and first responders are heartwarming. On the other hand, simple kind acts such as wearing a mask and social distancing are shunned by some in the name of political ideology or being tough.

Or some complain that such measures somehow invade their free choice as Americans, yet those same people are perfectly content to wear seat belts and motorcycle helmets, and they even comply with local store signs that say "no shirt, no shoes, no service." As the coronavirus began to spread again in the fall of 2020, I wondered what the results could have been if all Americans had simply decided to be kind and protect one another. Also, kindness need not involve money or much effort at all. The simple acts of holding a door or allowing a fellow commuter to merge into traffic can go a long way toward making our world a better place.

As a final thought, kindness must be genuine; it cannot be faked. I have an acquaintance who is a retired senior general officer. His personal style is to profusely praise and compliment everyone in his path, almost to the point of being nauseating. Those who know him, though, recognize that this flattery is not genuine. What my friend fails to realize is that constantly telling people how great they are, even when it's not true, has the opposite effect because people can see it for what it is. In other words, telling me the shine on my shoes looks great after I have walked through a puddle of mud is not being kind, it's being disingenuous. Coleman Cox said, "Spend five minutes every day thinking of some good you can do someone— then do it."[11]

Final Thoughts

It has been said that we are the sum of our life experiences and the people we have met. I have had great life experiences and have met incredible people. I am indeed leading a blessed life. When I entered first grade and discovered how far behind I was in the curriculum, my life's journey thus far was inconceivable. Achieving the military grade of four-star general is entry into an exclusive club. Even in retirement, I am still accorded by many the title of general. But in many ways I am still that eighteen-year-old airman who graduated from basic military training in 1972. I've since learned to play golf but would rather not, and I don't drink or smoke cigars like many of my military counterparts did. I remain most comfortable wearing a pair of jeans and a sweatshirt, and my beverage of choice is a McDonald's large iced tea. For relaxation, I prefer walking my dog in a local park or waxing my 1972 Chevrolet Monte Carlo over a luxury cruise or dining in a fancy restaurant.

We live in an amazing country. America really is the greatest country on earth. Whether we are born to affluent parents who can provide every advantage in education and resources or reared in an inner-city or rural area with poor living conditions and substandard schools, in America, either can achieve their dreams of prosperity and success. That doesn't mean there will not be obstacles to overcome, but with persistence, hard work, and determination, in America we can in fact achieve anything.

That's my career and life in a nutshell. I was born a dark horse. My living conditions were poor and my education was subpar, but those factors could not and did not deter me. The revelation that I was born with at least as much potential as everyone else did not come easy, but it eventually came. Did I have to work harder than some others to fulfill my potential? Maybe. But I know there are many others that had to work even harder. Like my father and his father, I had to learn to play the hand life dealt me. I had to figure out my strengths and capitalize on them. I also had to recognize my weaknesses and improve on them.

I wrote this memoir to capture and summarize my journey from the Horseshoe to the Pentagon, with the hope that it might inspire others to realize their potential. So the reality is that this memoir is not about me at all. Rather, it's about my family, which has been so supportive of every endeavor I attempted. It's also about the hundreds of people who helped and supported me over the years. I have had great bosses, mentors, and subordinates, and I am so grateful for their encouragement and support.

From Chief Master Sergeant Brown, who helped me achieve acceptance into OTS, to Col. Frank Tuck, who provided a strong initial foundation to an eager and enthusiastic second lieutenant. From Gen. Hal Hornburg, who set a stellar example, mentored me, and opened doors of opportunity, both during and after my Air Force career, to Adm. Mike Mullen, who gave me the opportunity to prove myself in a tough arena on the Joint Staff. And Air Force chief of staff Gen. Norty

Schwartz and Air Force Secretary Michael Donley, who took a chance on a nontra-ditional pick, promoted me to four stars, and made me the thirty-seventh vice chief of staff of the Air Force. I was blessed over my career with great leaders who gave me unwavering support and who, ironically, did not look like me.

It has been said that there are two ways to live your life: as though nothing is a miracle, or as though everything is a miracle. My life has been a succession of miracles. In the Bible, the book of John, chapter 9, describes a wonderful story of Jesus healing a man that had been blind from birth. The Pharisees were upset because Jesus purportedly performed this miracle on the Sabbath day, which was against their religious law. Incredulous over the breach of a sacred commandment, the Pharisees attempted to discredit Jesus by questioning the once blind man to secure a confession that Jesus was a sinner. The gentleman who gained his sight responded, "Whether he is a sinner or not, I do not know. One thing I do know, I was blind, but now I see." I cannot fully comprehend or explain my journey from the Horseshoe to the Pentagon. But one thing I do know: I was an inner-city youth labeled as a dark horse who endured the journey to become a four-star general in the Pentagon.

Notes

Preface

1. Maya Angelou, *Rainbow in the Cloud: The Wisdom and Spirit of Maya Angelou* (New York: Random House, 2014), 41.

Chapter 1. The Horseshoe

1. Tupac Shakur, interview by Sway on KMEL's westside radio program, transcribed by Davey D., April 19, 1996.
2. Kareem Abdul-Jabbar, *Giant Steps* (New York: Bantam Books, 1983), 16.
3. Associated Press, "Oprah Reflects on History of African Americans on TV," May 14, 2014, https://pagesix.com/2015/05/14/oprah-relects-on-history-of-african-americans-on-tv/.

Chapter 2. Red House

1. Governor Rick Perry during a speech at the Saturday night Red State gathering of conservative activists, where he announced his presidential campaign, Waterloo, Iowa, August 14, 2011.

Chapter 3. Fish Out of Water

1. Kumail Nanjiani, from a commencement speech at Grinnell College, Iowa, May 22, 2017.

Chapter 4. Enlisted during the 1970s

1. Marvin Gaye, "Inner City Blues (Make Me Wanna Holler)," from the album *What's Going On*, 1971.

Chapter 5. An Officer and a Gentleman

1. Gen. Hugh Shelton, interview on *Larry King Live*, CNN, October 1, 2001.

Chapter 6. Full Bird

1. Gen. George S. Patton, *War As I Knew It* (Boston: Houghton Mifflin, 1947), 357.
2. Lt. Col. Charles M. Bussey, *Firefight at Yechon: Courage and Racism in the Korean War* (Washington, DC: Brassey's, 1991), 225–26.
3. Benjamin Jowett, *Thucydides*, 2nd ed. (Oxford: Oxford University Press, 1900), 205.

Chapter 7. Rarefied Air

1. Peter Drucker, *Managing for the Future* (New York: Routledge, 1992), 99.
2. Gen. Colin Powell, interview with Kaleth Wright, chief master sergeant of the Air Force, on "The New Normal," June 16, 2020, https://www.youtube.com/watch?v=ZG4eb5oX2bw.

Chapter 8. #37

1. Gen. Colin Powell (Ret.), e-mail to the author, December 20, 2020.
2. John A. Stokes, with Lois Wolfe and Herman J. Viola, *Students on Strike: Jim Crow, Civil Rights, Brown and Me: A Memoir* (Washington, D.C.: National Geographic, 2008), 9.
3. Stephen Frazier, "John Lewis: 'I thought I was going to die,'" CNN.com/U.S. May 10, 2001, https://edition.cnn.com/2001/US/05/10/access.lewis.freedom.rides/ (April 3, 2018).
4. Stephen Losey, "Hear JFK Rant about 'Silly Bastard' in the Air Force," *Air Force Times*, March 12, 2014, http://flightlines.airforcetimes.com/2014/03/12/hear-jfk-rant-about-silly-bastard-in-the-air-force/ (May 8, 2017).
5. Mark Thompson, "The Roots of Sexual Abuse in the Military," statement by President Obama at a White House meeting with military leaders, *Time,* May 17, 2013, https://nation.time.com/2013/05/17/the-roots-of-sexual-abuse-in-the-military/, (November 4, 2018).

Chapter 9. Changing Lanes

1. President Woodrow Wilson during an address to Salesmanship Congress in Detroit, July 10, 1916.

Chapter 10. Life Lessons

1. Ralph Waldo Emerson, "The Conduct of Life," in *The Complete Works of Ralph Waldo Emerson*, vol. VI (Boston: Houghton Mifflin, 1903–4), 99.

2. Unknown, www.wordquote.com/in-my-life-ive-lived-ive-loved-ive-lost/, May 12, 2019.

3. Coleman Cox, *Listen to This* (San Francisco: Coleman Cox Publishing, 1922).

4. John Wooden and Steve Jamison, *Wooden on Leadership* (New York: McGraw-Hill, 2005).

5. Heather Long and Andrew Van Dam, "The Black-White Economic Divide Is as Wide as It Was in 1968," *Washington Post*, June 4, 2020.

6. Long and Van Dam, "The Black-White Economic Divide."

7. Long and Van Dam, "The Black-White Economic Divide."

8. Joshua Bote, "'Get in good trouble, necessary trouble:' Rep. John Lewis in His Own Words," *USA Today*, July 19, 2020.

9. Maureen Stearns, *Conscious Courage: Turning Everyday Challenges into Opportunities* (St. Petersburg, FL: Enrichment Books, 2004).

10. Gen. Lloyd "Fig" Newton (Ret.), telephone interview, April 10, 2019.

11. Coleman Cox, *Take It From Me* (San Francisco: Coleman Cox Publishing, 1921).

Bibliography

☆ ☆ ☆ ☆

Abdul-Jabbar, Kareem. *Giant Steps.* New York: Bantam Books, 1983.

Angelou, Maya. *Rainbow in the Cloud: The Wisdom and Spirit of Maya Angelou.* New York: Random House Books, 2014.

Associated Press. "Oprah Reflects on History of African Americans on TV." Page Six. May 14, 2015. https://pagesix.com/2015/05/14/oprah-relects-on-history-of -african-americans-on-tv/.

Bote, Joshua. "'Get in trouble, necessary trouble': Rep. John Lewis in His Own Words." *USA Today.* July 19, 2020. https://www.usatoday.com/story/news/politics /2020/07/18/rep-lewis/most-memorable-quotes.

Bussey, Charles. *Firefight at Yechon: Courage and Racism in the Korean War.* Washington, D.C.: Brassey's, 1991.

Cox, Coleman. *Listen to This.* San Francisco: Coleman Cox Publishing, 1922.

———. *Take it From Me.* San Francisco: Coleman Cox Publishing, 1921.

Drucker, Peter. *Managing for the Future.* New York: Routledge, 1992.

Emerson, Ralph Waldo. "The Conduct of Life." In *The Complete Works of Ralph Waldo Emerson*, vol. VI. Boston: Houghton Mifflin, 1903–4.

Frazier, Stephen. "John Lewis: 'I thought I was going to die.'" CNN. May 10, 2001. https://edition.cnn.com/2001/US/05/10/access.lewis.freedom.rides/.

Gaye, Marvin. "Inner City Blues (Make Me Wanna Holler)." From the album *What's Going On*, 1971.

Jowett, Benjamin. *Thucydides.* 2nd ed. Oxford: Oxford University Press, 1990.

Long, Heather, and Andrew Van Dam. "The Black-White Economic Divide Is as Wide as It Was in 1968." *Washington Post.* June 4, 2020.

Losey, Stephen. "Hear JFK Rant about 'Silly Bastard' in the Air Force." *Air Force Times*. March 12, 2014. http://flightlines.airforcetimes.com/2014/03/12/hear-jfk-rant-about-silly-bastard-in-the-air-force/.

Nanjiani, Kumail. From a commencement speech at Grinnell College, Iowa. May 22, 2017.

Newton, Lloyd, Gen. Telephone interview. April 10, 2019.

Patton, George S., Gen. *War as I Knew It*. Boston: Houghton Mifflin, 1947.

Perry, Rick. During a speech at the Saturday night Red State gathering of conservative activists, where he announced his presidential campaign. Waterloo, Iowa. August 14, 2011.

Powell, Colin, Gen. (Ret.). Interview with Kaleth Wright, chief master sergeant of the Air Force, on "The New Normal." June 16, 2020. https://www.youtube.com/watch?v=ZG4eb5oX2bw.

———. Email to the author. December 20, 2020.

Shakur, Tupac. Interview by Sway on KMEL's westside radio program. Transcribed by Davey D. April 19, 1996.

Shelton, Hugh, Gen. (Ret.). *Larry King Live* interview. CNN. October 1, 2001.

Stearns, Maureen. *Conscious Courage: Turning Everyday Challenges into Opportunities*. St. Petersburg, FL: Enrichment Books, 2004.

Stokes, John A., with Lois Wolfe and Herman J. Viola. *Students on Strike: Jim Crow, Civil Rights, Brown and Me*. Washington, D.C.: National Geographic Society. 2008.

Thompson, Mark. "The Roots of Sexual Abuse in the Military." Statement by President Obama at a White House meeting with military leaders. *Time*. May 17, 2013. https://nation.time.com/2013/05/17/the-roots-of-sexual-abuse-in-the-military/. November 4, 2018.

Unknown. https://www.wordquote.com/in-my-life-ive-lived-ive-loved-ive-lost/. December 17, 2018.

Wilson, Woodrow. During an address to Salesmanship Congress in Detroit. July 10, 1916.

Wooden, John, and Steve Jamison. *Wooden on Leadership*. New York: McGraw-Hill, 2005.

About the Author

☆ ☆ ☆ ☆

Gen. Larry Spencer, USAF (Ret.), was born and raised in Washington, D.C. Spencer enlisted in the U.S. Air Force in 1971, completed his bachelor of science degree, and was commissioned as a second lieutenant in 1980. Spencer quickly climbed the ranks, culminating as the 37th Vice Chief of Staff of the Air Force. He later became president of the Air Force Association and is now president of the Armed Forces Benefit Association/5Star Life Insurance Company.

The Naval Institute Press is the book-publishing arm of the U.S. Naval Institute, a private, nonprofit, membership society for sea service professionals and others who share an interest in naval and maritime affairs. Established in 1873 at the U.S. Naval Academy in Annapolis, Maryland, where its offices remain today, the Naval Institute has members worldwide.

Members of the Naval Institute support the education programs of the society and receive the influential monthly magazine *Proceedings* or the colorful bimonthly magazine *Naval History* and discounts on fine nautical prints and on ship and aircraft photos. They also have access to the transcripts of the Institute's Oral History Program and get discounted admission to any of the Institute-sponsored seminars offered around the country.

The Naval Institute's book-publishing program, begun in 1898 with basic guides to naval practices, has broadened its scope to include books of more general interest. Now the Naval Institute Press publishes about seventy titles each year, ranging from how-to books on boating and navigation to battle histories, biographies, ship and aircraft guides, and novels. Institute members receive significant discounts on the Press's more than eight hundred books in print.

Full-time students are eligible for special half-price membership rates. Life memberships are also available.

For a free catalog describing Naval Institute Press books currently available, and for further information about joining the U.S. Naval Institute, please write to:

Member Services
U.S. NAVAL INSTITUTE
291 Wood Road
Annapolis, MD 21402-5034
Telephone: (800) 233-8764
Fax: (410) 571-1703
Web address: www.usni.org